STATE
CONSTITUTIONAL
CONVENTIONS

STATE CONSTITUTIONAL CONVENTIONS

1959-1975

A Bibliography

compiled by
SUSAN RICE YARGER

introduction by
RICHARD H. LEACH
Professor of Political Science,
Duke University

GREENWOOD PRESS
Westport, Conn. • London, England

Library of Congress Cataloging in Publication Data

Yarger, Susan Rice.
  State constitutional conventions, 1959-1975.

  Supplements and updates C. E. Browne's State constitutional
conventions from independence to the completion of the
present Union, 1776-1959.
  1. Constitutional conventions—United States—States—
Bibliography. 2. Constitutions, State—United States—Bibliography. I. Browne, Cynthia E. State constitutional conventions from independence to the completion of the present
Union, 1776-1959. II. Title.
KF4501.Y37   016.342'73'024   75-40939
  ISBN: 0-8371-8683-8

Library of Congress Catalog Card Number: 75-40939
ISBN: 0-8371-8683-8

First published in 1976

Greenwood Press, a division of Williamhouse-Regency Inc.
51 Riverside Avenue, Westport, Connecticut 06880

Printed in the United States of America

Contents

Preface

Included in this collection are all publications of state constitutional conventions, commissions, and legislative or executive committees, and all special studies prepared for the convention or commission bodies. For this series we have only included documentation for those states that brought the results of their endeavors to the electorate, regardless of the final outcome.

As in the earlier Greenwood Press collection, we found that the quantity and quality of published material varied widely from state to state, and we found it impossible to include some recent efforts because work is still in progress. Two of the most recent constitutional revision efforts (Louisiana and Texas) have yet to be edited and published. The New Jersey and New Mexico materials, although emanating from earlier conventions, also remain in a preparatory state.

The documents selected for the collection were generally of an official, noninterpretive nature, such as, enabling legislation, proceedings, journals, resolutions, and rules, public hearings, the proposed constitution, and the constitution as revised and implemented by the electorate. Exception to "noninterpretive" materials was made for the many special studies commissioned by the various conventions.

The program covers the last sixteen years in state legislative history. Generally the documents are arranged chronologically by date of publication and within a particular date by issuing sequence or numbering scheme of the special reports that were published. Constitutions as amended and issued prior to the calling of the convention, the proposed constitution issued before the referendum, and the constitution as ratified by the electorate were included, wherever possible. The constitution as amended prior to the convention was not included if there had been no changes in the text presented in the earlier Greenwood program.

The bibliography was developed through use of the Library of Congress card catalog, published bibliographies of a general nature and those pertaining to individual states. Librarians in our state libraries were consulted for bibliographic assistance; their generous advice and cooperation made this project possible.

Susan Rice Yarger
Germantown, Maryland

Introduction

STATE CONSTITUTIONAL
CONVENTIONS AND COMMISSIONS: 1959-1975*

Richard H. Leach
Professor of Political Science
Duke University

> State constitutions, for so long the drag anchors of state progress, and permanent cloaks for the protection of special interests and points of view, should be revised or rewritten into more concise statements of principle.
>
> Terry Sanford, *Storm Over the States* (1967)

*These introductory remarks draw heavily from the section in successive editions of the Council of State Government's *The Book of the States* on "State Constitutions and Constitutional Revision." No other source provides as careful and complete coverage as these biennial reviews. They should be consulted for more detailed analysis of many of the points made here and their bibliographies relied on to supplement the official publications in the bibliography that follows these remarks. The analysis of state constitutional revision in W. Brooke Graves, *American State Government* 4th ed. (Boston, 1953), Chapter 3, is still relevant and incisive.

The importance of the role state constitutions play in American government hardly needs emphasis. State constitutions underlie that segment of the American governmental whole which most intimately affects our lives. If the states are not concerned with grand international strategy, with the overall economy, or with broad issues of civil rights (to cite only three areas of national governmental concern) the states -- and the local governments they create and support -- affect most directly the interwoven educational, legal, cultural, recreational, social, and economic framework within which Americans structure their patterns of daily living. Understanding state constitutions is thus the first step toward understanding the process of domestic self-government in the United States.

Massachusetts and New Hampshire first utilized the convention device to write their original state constitutions in 1779, and its use both to draw up the first constitution of a territory-turned-state and to propose changes in that document has become standard practice in the United States. So standard, indeed, that the constitutions of 39 states provide specifically for calling conventions for that purpose, and even where that is not the case, legislative authority to do so has been established in practice. Since the first round in the 1820s, over 200 constitutional conventions in the states have been convened to make changes required in the fundamental state law by effecting changes in the body politic itself. The period from 1959 to 1975 has been a particularly active one for constitutional revision, as a growing number of constitutional commissions joined with the traditional conventions in what Charles R. Adrian has called a "revival of constitution writing" after the war.[1]

Though the term "constitutional commission" is used loosely to describe a variety of groups involved in constitutional revision, the true constitutional commission is usually an ad hoc body, "normally composed of both official and lay citizen appointees, having constitutional revision as their paramount concern." They are ordinarily created by statute, by legislative resolution, or by executive order, though the new constitution of Florida, which went into effect in 1969, gives constitutional status to a commission as a formal means of suggesting constitutional change.[2] The bodies cometimes act in lieu of a convention; they are sometimes employed as "an educational device to stir up interest in...revision, in the hope that in time a convention may be called"; and sometimes they are used as a sort or preparatory body "to identify problems and carry on preliminary work for a convention."[3] Their recent popularity "is attributable largely to their general acceptability to state legislators, who may accept, reject, or modify in whole or in part commission recommendations."[4] Besides a frequent difference in purpose, they differ from conventions chiefly in that members of a convention are delegates of the people, specially elected to perform their constituent function, and that the organization of and procedures to be observed by conventions usually are more carefully detailed in the authorizing act.

Both are now common features on the state scene. Their presence there reflects a compelling need for constitutional revision both to work into the constitution some recognition of shifts in the pattern of dominant interests in the state that have taken place and to build on the increasing evidence that there are more efficient and effective ways to accomplish state business.

To be sure, much of this can be -- and is -- accomplished by use of the constitutional initiative in the dozen or so states that allow it or by amendment in all the states. Indeed, while many state constitutions limit the use of these devices to one specific subject at a time and do not permit changes introduced thereby to apply to related matter in other parts of the constitution, in other states a single amendment may serve as the vehicle for proposing a complete new constitution, as it recurred in Florida in 1968.[5] It is even possible to modernize an entire constitution by a series of amendments over time, which is what California has been doing since 1966 and what South Carolina, South Dakota, and Minnesota are making progress with. These latter possibilities are the exception, however; for the most part the amendment process at best results in piecemeal change and represents the triumph of narrow pressures rather than of the public interest. Nor does it leave behind a clear record of attention and discussion. Because it does not give insight into the constituent process, consideration of change by amendment has not been included in the present analysis. It remains, however, the most traveled route to constitutional change in use by the American states today.

The purpose of this essay is to look in some detail at the central issues that have generated constitutional revision by conventions and commissions in the states since about 1959, to see how the several conventions and commissions involved in that process over the fifteen-year period were organized and went about their work, to review the major substantive areas of change they recommended, and to come to some conclusions about the impact of those bodies on the practices of state and local government in the United States today.

I

As the quotation from Terry Sanford used at the beginning of this essay suggests, part of the chronic need for state constitutional revision lies in the age of many of the state constitutions themselves, which, despite a great number of amendments to many, tends to make them unsuitable bases from which to tackle today's problems, to say nothing about meeting those of tomorrow. The age of American state constitutions, in fact, is quite remarkable, as Table 1 suggests.

Table 1. Effective Date of American State Constitutions

Before 1800	1800-1850	1850-1875
Massachusetts	Maine[a]	Arkansas
New Hampshire	Rhode Island	Indiana
Vermont	Wisconsin	Iowa
		Kansas
		Maryland
		Minnesota
		Nebraska
		Nevada
		Ohio
		Tennessee
		Oregon
		West Virginia

Table 1. Continued

1875-1900	1900-1940	1940-1974
California	Alabama	Alaska
Colorado	Arizona	Connecticut
Delaware	Louisiana	Florida
Idaho	New Mexico	Georgia
Kentucky	Oklahoma	Hawaii
Mississippi		Illinois
New York		Michigan
North Dakota		Missouri
South Carolina		Montana
South Dakota		New Jersey
Texas		North Carolina[b]
Utah		Pennsylvania
Washington		Virginia
Wyoming		

[a] Recodified by the Chief Justice under special authority in 1951 and 1965.

[b] Basically the 1868 document editorially revised.

Source: The Statesman's Year-Book 1974-1975 (London, 1974), pp. 589-713.

But the age of the constitutions was not, by itself, responsible for the wave of interest in constitutional revision which culminated in the 1960s. That wave resulted in part from the cumulative effect of years of effort to justify and secure revision. The impact of the National Municipal League's work in particular was important. From the publication of the first edition of its Model State Constitution in 1921, it pushed through a research and publication program for constitutional revision. It not only pointed up the issues to be dealt with by those who were successful in initiating the revision process in their states, but provided extensive background material for them to utilize and even showed them how to mount a convention effort and shape the final product thereof.[6] Other groups[7] and individuals[8] contributed their share, with the result that revising constitutions came to be seen much more generally than ever before "as essential to the future health and well-being of the states."[9] By the early sixties, interest in state constitutional revision had begun to be evident in an increasing number of gubernatorial messages to legislatures and the public, in the activities of a good many citizens' groups that took up the cause, and in the research and publications of a large number of academic and other writers. The decade of the sixties, indeed, was to see state constitutional revision become almost a fad.

Another compelling reason for the rising tide of interest in constitutional revision in the states was the situation created by the U.S. Supreme Court's decisions on reapportionment in 1962 and 1964. Not only was constitutional change necessary to meet the new "one-man, one-vote" requirement, but, as John Bebout observed, the Court's action served to remove or reduce "opposition to general constitutional revision by those who formerly feared that it would open the

door to alteration" of apportionment patterns.[10] With their worst
fears realized, other changes did not seem so bad.

Also contributing its share to the drive for constitutional revision was a widespread kindling of interest in the improvement of
state and local government as twentieth-century developments required more and more governmental intervention. These included "rapid
urbanization with its attendant problems, population growth and mo-
bility, technological and development, growing pressures for equal
treatment for minority groups, and ever-increasing insistence on
higher and better living standards in an affluent society."[11] The
limits of the federal government's power to deal with all these developments were always acknowledged, but they were made especially
evident in the 1960s. The possibility that these needs could be met
by the antiquated governmental structure and processes of many of the
states, however, did not seem great. The reports of the Commission
of Intergovernmental Relations, known as the Kestnbaum Commission, in
the middle and late fifties, reflected these developments and showed
how much the future of America itself depended on reviving the vigor
and effectiveness of state and local government. The commission's work
was followed by an outpouring of literature on state and local government reform from such prestigious groups as the Committee for Economic Development, the National Governors' Conference, the Council of
State Governments, and the Public Administration Service of Chicago.[12]
It did no harm either to the swelling pressure for constitutional
change across the nation that the states of Alaska and Hawaii were
just then working on their first state constitutions. In many ways,
the changes and innovations these states were making provided both
a challenge and a stimulus for the other states. In any case, the
possibility of continuing to creak along under constitutions designed
for another day began to wear thin, and the door to constitutional
revision was opened wide.

Or so it seemed from the number of states in which calls for
constitutional conventions and commissions began to be made. But the
enthusiasm for change had not reached the grass roots in some states,
with the result that formal calls for conventions were voted down in
a good many states right through the period. Where success was achieved,
it came usually after a good deal of hard work in getting popular
support for the idea. The experience in Michigan in launching its
revision effort in 1961, which was led by the Junior Chamber of Commerce and the League of Women Voters, later joined by an umbrella-
type group, Citizens for Michigan, was instructive to many other
states, as was the work done in Pennsylvania by A Modern Constitution
for Pennsylvania, Inc.

Unfortunately, there are no readily available statistics on the
exact number of constitutional conventions and commissions held between 1959 and 1975. Not until The Book of the States 1970-1971 issue
did even that comprehensive catalogue of what goes on in the states
begin to carry data about conventions and commissions. An earlier
edition was content with declaring that approximately one-third of the
states were "more or less actively" engaged in some kind of revision
activity in the 1959-1961 biennium, while during the 1968-1969 biennium at least thirty-four states had taken some action "directed
toward the general revision of their basic instruments of government."[13]

Much of this effort had no official outcome, but between 1960

and 1967 there were constitutional commissions in Arkansas, Califor-
nia, Florida, Georgia, Hawaii, Idaho, Illinois, Kansas, Kentucky,
Louisiana, Maryland, Michigan, Nebraska, New Jersey, New Mexico,
New York, North Dakota, Oregon, Pennsylvania, Rhode Island, Texas,
Washington, and Wisconsin, and constitutional conventions in Connec-
ticut, Maryland, Michigan, New Jersey, New Hampshire, New York, Rhode
Island, and Tennessee. Table 2 gives the statistics for the period
from 1968 to 1973.

Table 2. Number of State Constitutional Conventions
and Commissions 1968-1973, by Bienni

	1968-69	1970-71	1972-73
Conventions	7	5	4
Commissions	22	13	11

Source: The Book of the States 1970-1971, Table 4; 1972-1973 and
1974-1975, Table 1. These tables give the dates, type, vote
on the referenda calling the conventions, nature of the preparatory body, appropriation, number of delegates, convention
proposals, and outcome of referenda on the proposals of the
convention for conventions, and the name, method and date of
creation, period of operation, membership number and type,
funding, purpose, and proposals and actions for commissions.

II

This essay is not the place to describe in detail what went on in
each of the foregoing conventions and commissions. Use of the bibliography will yield that knowledge. A number of general comments might be
made about the creation and the organization and procedures of those
bodies, however, before the issues they discussed are summarized and
the impact of their proposals assessed. It might first be noted that
state constitutional activity between 1959 and 1975 was to a greater
degree than ever before the result of federal judicial pressure, if
not federal judicial order. Not enough attention has been paid to
this development in the practice of American federalism to enable its
effects to be analyzed. But it at least raises questions about the
autonomy of the states over their own constitution, a principle
that would seem to be at the heart of the concept of federalism. Not
all the judicial pressure came from the federal level. The New Jersey
State Supreme Court, for example, precipitated the New Jersey Constitutional Convention of 1966. Perhaps in reaction to such pressure
in a number of states, consideration of constitutional revision was
limited, as in Connecticut, to the specific matters defined by the
courts. Where this was the case, it may have worked a hardship on
opening the whole constitution to general revision. In other states,
as in Maryland for example, the necessity of acting on apportionment
capped years, if not decades, of efforts to get general constitutional revision under way and finally brought the opportunity to do so.
Secondly, it is worth noting that the official work of the con-

ventions and commissions was preceded or accompanied in a number of
cases by some remarkable work by unofficial groups, without which
the official bodies would have been much the poorer. Thus before the
1967 New York Convention, "Columbia University's Academy of Political
Science followed a precedent it had established prior to the constitutional convention of 1915 and devoted its Proceedings to a series
of papers on the various procedural and substantive aspects of constitutional convention of 1915 and devoted its Proceedings to a series
of papers on the various procedural and substantive aspects of constitutional revision."[14] In Louisiana, the Louisiana State Law Institute performed much the same role before its 1973 convention, and
in Pennsylvania, the Pennsylvania Bar Association proposed a series
of changes before the 1965 convention convened in that state.

A third point to make is that the constitutional work of the
sixties and early seventies could probably be done more carefully
than had been customary earlier. Not only could it draw from the
work of such groups as the National Municipal League, but it was
able to utilize experts as it went along. Most of the acts calling
conventions and commissions into being specifically provided for the
employment of consultants and/or staff, and in most cases the state
legislature supported the authorization with an appropriation to pay
for them. Professor Sturm reports that the average total funding for
commissions in the 1970-71 biennium, for instance, was $96,587, with
a median between $75,000 and $80,000, while the average in the 1972-73
biennium was $269,159, with a median of $162,084.[15] The total appropriation to defray the expenses of the Illinois Convention of 1969
was $2.88 million and for the Louisiana Convention of 1973, $2.94
million. The bulk of these monies went for research and analysis. On
the other hand, though the Texas House of Representatives passed a
resolution creating a Constitutional Revision Study Commission in
1967, it did not go on to appropriate any state funds in support of
it, so that the funding had to come from private sources. Earlier
the funds for the preparatory work and even for the physical facili-
ties to house the Michigan convention of 1961 had been granted by
the W. K. Kellogg Foundation.

Most observers agreed that the personnel of the conventions and
commissions between 1960 and 1974 was quite highly qualified, reflecting a determination on the part of the states to have a real go
at constitutional revision. While it cannot be demonstrated that
every member of a constitutional commission was as well qualified as
those of the Kentucky Constitutional Revision Assembly of 1964 (or
even that the surface qualifications of those appointees was matched
in fact by their performance!), that membership was not an unusual
occurrence in the period. The fifty members of the Assembly had "a
rich and varied background in government and law. Of seven former
governors who [were] members, five [were] lawyers and three [had] been
judges of the Court of Appeals. The forty-three others -- forty-one
men and two women -- include[d] twenty-five lawyers, four bankers,
several from the field of education, the remainder from miscellaneous
occupations. Four delegates serve[d] or ha[d] served in the United
States Senate. Four...on the State Court of Appeals, three on the State
Circuit Court, ten in the General Assembly. Eight ha[d] rendered other
significant public service at the state level, none at the local level."[16]

While the "quality" of delegates to a convention is not likely to be as uniform as those appointed to commissions, inasmuch as they are elected from the body of the people as a whole, the membership lists of most conventions carreid the names of some of the state's most prominent citizens, and most conventions distinguished themselves by choosing well-qualified officers. The Maryland Convention of 1967, for example, chose as its president the man who had previously served as chairman of the state's constitutional commission.

In other ways the experience of the past, and the experience that accumulated during the period, helped the constitutional bodies in the sixties and early seventies perform at a high level of competence. Most of the enabling acts for conventions and commissions provided that the members should be paid at a level that would pretty well guarantee that they put their full attention to the work at hand. A number of states set compensation and allowances for members of commissions and conventions at the same rates as for members of the state legislature, which, at least in the case of the members of the New York Convention of 1967, was $15,000 per annum. The Maryland Convention of the same year organized and selected its committees "without regard to party affiliation. And to minimize both partisanship and parochialism, delegates were seated alphabetically."[17] The Pennsylvania Convention of 1967-68 did much the same thing. The relatively long duration of many of the conventions and commissions may also speak to their diligence.

The Montana Convention of 1971-72 began with a two-day orientation period, followed by a three-day organizational meeting, thus enabling the delegates to have established some working knowledge of what they were about and some working relationships before they moved on to the substance of reform.

Finally, some comment needs to be made with regard to the concern for public participation demonstrated by many of the commissions and conventions. Not every group did what the Rhode Island Convention of 1964-65 did, which was to invite "all qualified electors to submit proposals for its consideration"[18] (perhaps since it was Rhode Island's first unlimited convention in 122 years, the delegates felt a special urgency to solicit public input!), or as the North Dakota Convention of 1971 did, which was to set up a special Hearing Committee, which conducted public hearings throughout the state "to learn the 'grass roots' opinion about what the new constitution should contain and to bring the convention to the people." In addition, the rules adopted by the North Dakota Convention "permitted individuals to submit their personal proposals to appropriate committees for consideration."[19] Even so, observers of the constitutional revision bodies during the period agree that the proceedings were generally characterized by a remarkable degree of free and open discussion, much of it directly reflecting public ideas and convictions.

Of course, to a great extent the possibilities of a commission or convention are outlined by the terms of the enabling act or executive terms of reference which brought the body into being. There is to be found not only the prescription of how many members or delegates there will be, how they will be chosen, and whom they are to represent, but much about how they will work once they are together.

If the legislature makes the wrong prescription -- if it calls for too many or too few delegates for example, or it is too stingy with appropriations -- the revision body may be handicapped from the outset in meeting expectations. There is probably no universally applicable enabling act; each is the peculiar product of a particular time and set of circumstances. But two or three may be illustrative of what they provide.

The act enabling the Connecticut Convention of 1964 provided for a strictly limited convention; attention was only to be directed to four specific matters. It called for the election of 84 delegates, to be equally divided between the two major political parties in the state.[20] It required the vote of two-thirds of the whole membership to pass a measure. It authorized the convention to issue subpoenas and employ consultants and staff. It provided an appropriation of $500,000 to meet the convention's expenses, to be paid out through the governor's office. In setting up the constitutional convention of 1966 the New Jersey legislature provided that the election of delegates be held on March 1 and those running were to be nominated by parties but with the restriction that no party might elect more than half of the delegates from any one county. The delegates elected were required to meet on March 21 and to take action by June. A weighted-vote system was to be used, the total 112 votes to be distributed among the counties on a population basis. The convention's recommendations were to be submitted to the electorate for approval. The Idaho act of 1965 authorizing the commission on constitutional revision in that state provided for a fifteen-member body -- five to be appointed by the Governor, five by the Chief Justice of the State Supreme Court, and five by the Legislative Council. An organizational meeting was required to be held before September 1. The commission was made responsible for making a thorough study and review of the existing Idaho constitution and for reporting its findings and recommendations to the legislature by December 1, 1966.

Particularly important in the enabling specifications is what kind of convention is called for. Some conventions, as already noted, are limited in their authority to propose changes, as was the Pennsylvania Convention of 1967. Most of the conventions during the period under consideration here, however, were not so limited; they were free to open all the existing constitution up to examination and, indeed, expected to do so. Pennsylvania, it should be noted, experimented with a dual approach that may become widely used in the future: the legislature (with the aid of a constitutional commission) framed certain reforms into constitutional amendments to refer to the people and assigned other areas to the limited convention for consideration and recommendation.

As mentioned earlier in this essay, Article XI of the 1969 Florida constitution provides for the establishment of a thirty-seven member constitutional revision commission to be appointed ten years after its adoption (i.e., in 1979) and then every twentieth year thereafter to study the state constitution and to propose the revision of all or any part of it. Article XI provides that the State Attorney-General shall be a member and that the others be appointed by various state officials. It is the only constitution to date that contains this kind of detailed requirement. Ordinarily constitutions provide only for constitutional conventions and then merely give the conditions for issuing a convention call.

Finally, how conventions and commissions are expected to make their recommendations is important. So many rejections of whole new constitutions by the voters in the early years of the period from 1959 to 1975 was undoubtedly a major factor in leading other states to decide "to seek constitutional reform gradually through a series of steps." Thus whereas the Rhode Island, Maryland, and New Mexico conventions all submitted a new constitution as a single proposition to their voters, who rejected all of them, the Pennsylvania and Hawaii conventions were allowed to present "their recommendations in the form of a series of proposals that could be voted on separately ...."[21] The Hawaii voters, indeed, were given the option of either approving all the propositions by a single vote or voting on each proposition separately. All the recommendations made by these two conventions were approved, except one proposition in Hawaii.

Thus some of the range of effectiveness of conventions and commissions is set at the beginning in terms of how the body is constructed and what limitation is placed upon it. Since constitutions are, after all, political documents, playing as such a major role in the allocation of power and scarce societal resources,[22] constitutional revision bodies are inevitably political bodies. No matter how carefully they are put together, they reflect a variety of opposing viewpoints, and their decisions will favor some groups over others. Thus much of their success cannot be foretold but depends on what kind of a contest takes place during their considerations. John Straayer reminds us that this political role played by revision bodies helps to explain why such bodies are so often "the site of hot debate and competition, and why newly drafted documents are sometimes rejected at the polls. Whenever the subject of a new constitution is opened up, versted interests will fight for inclusion of provisions that would similarly benefit them."[23] If the fights are bitter, and many of them are, the proceedings necessarily affect the outcome, although it is not possible to pinpoint just where and how. In any case, the issues before the commission or convention are just as important as the structure and organization of the body in producing the final outcome.

III

The issues demanding attention in the process of constitutional revision generally have been brewing for some time. As noted earlier, they are usually the products of a rapidly changing society and represent shifts in focus in the body politic. All of them, as just suggested, have their strong proponents and opponents. It is not surprising how persistent some of the issues are when it is recalled that such central problems of government as representation, organization, intergovernmental relations, and finance can never be finally settled in a dynamic society. Thus it is interesting to look at the issues of the time in a list printed in the National Municipal Review in October 1937. The list remains remarkably up-to-date.[24]

1. Reorganization of the state administrative departments, and a review of the merits of proposals for new departments.

2. Improvement of the functioning of the legislature, which is at the very core of the democratic process.
3. Reorganization of the judicial system, in order to provide more efficient machinery for the administration of justice.
4. City-county relations and the reorganization of the system of local government, including consolidation, reallocation of functions, long-range planning, and proper land utilization.
5. Popular control of government, including the short ballot principle and proportional representation.
6. Budgetary methods and procedure, including the possibility of provision for a capital outlay budget, a reserve fund, and an annual budget.
7. The question of the extent, method, and purposes of state aid to political subdivisions as well as the relation of this question to the tax burden on real estate.
8. An increasing burden of Federal taxes and overlapping of state levies with both Federal and local levies deserves careful study.
9. In view of extended Federal activity in the labor field, what should be the function of the states? Should unions be incorporated? Should "a bill of rights for labor" be written into the constitution?
10. Extensions of governmental activity in social welfare may well receive consideration. Should housing be dealt with in the construction, and if so, in what manner?

About all that needs to be added to that list is the issue of reapportionment to make it descriptive of the issues faced by the conventions and commissions from 1959 to 1975. Cast another way, those issues were as follows:

1. Reapportionment: The need to make the representative principle truly operative in the states.
2. Legislative reform: The need to replace a "cumbersome, unrepresentative legislature, inadequately staffed to perform the lawmaking function intelligently, with excessively restricted powers, often unresponsive to public needs, especially in urban areas, and subject to manipulation by selfish interests."[25]
3. Executive reform: The need for a stronger and more effective executive in lieu of "a disintegrated and enfeebled executive with power widely dispersed and responsibility divided among a large number of elective officials on all levels, and an administrative structure of great complexity featured by duplication, overlapping, inefficiency, and waste."

4. Judicial reform: The need for a judicial system instead of
                       a "diffused, complicated, and largely unco-
                       ordinated judiciary, often lacking indepen-
                       dence, with judges selected on a political
                       basis and frequently without professional
                       qualifications on the lower levels."
5. Changes in local government: The need to relax the "rigid re-
                       strictions on local government that seriously
                       impede home rule."
6. Fiscal changes: The need both to improve the fiscal pos-
                       sibilities of the states and to relieve the
                       excessive burdens on local government while
                       at the same time providing some relief for
                       the overburdened taxpayer.
7. Expanding the concept of natural rights and making the prin-
                       ciple of self-government more meaningful:
                       The need to recognize the development of
                       new areas of civil rights and to make the
                       task of the voter easier by getting rid of
                       the "long ballot, listing a bewildering
                       array of candidates and issues...."
8. Simplification of the constitutional text: The need to rid con-
                       stitutions "of a mass of detail...blurring
                       the distinction between constitutional and
                       statutory law, and necessitating frequent
                       amendments."

Each of these issues will be dealt with individually in the following paragraphs. A group of miscellaneous issues will be considered
together at the end of this section.

Reapportionment

A major criticism of state government for a long time had been the
underrepresentation of urban and suburban voters in state legislatures. As noted above, meeting judicial requirements of reapportionment was a primary cause of the flurry of constitutional change in
the sixties. Not all the states received such specific directions
from the bench as did Connecticut from the Federal District Court
sitting in Hartford, which in 1964 suggested in no uncertain terms
Connecticut forthwith call a constitutional convention whose purpose
would be "to formulate state constitutional provisions for districting in the Senate, apportioning the House, revising decennially the
structure of the General Assembly and amending the state constitution by a procedure not in contravention of the United States Constitution."[26] But most states, feeling the warmth of the judicial
breath on them, undertook to accomplish most of those objectives any-
how.

There is no uniformity to the apportionment recommendations made
by the various commissions and conventions. Some involved only slight
alterations of existing practices, as in Tennessee; others had to
provide for extensive change if they were to avoid direct judicial
orders themselves. Most of them attempted to incorporate the one-man,
one-vote principle in the place of some sort of guaranteed representation for cities and counties, which was common in early versions
of many constitutions. Perhaps the most controversial proposals cen-
tered around ways to guarantee future reapportionment. A common solution, as in the New Jersey Convention of 1966, was to recommend that
future apportionments be made by some sort of commission outside the
legislature itself.

Legislative Reform

As Professor Sturm has noted, "Since constitutions impose more
limitations on lawmaking bodies than on the other branches, the largest
number of [proposed] changes logically applied to legislatures."[27]
A great deal of the research done on state government and its improvement preceding and accompanying the revision efforts in the sixties had focused on the legislative problem, so that conventions
and commissions had before them a number of alternative possibilities.
Among those considered were the following: increasing legislative
pay and allowances set in constitutions, or, preferably, giving the
legislature authority to set its own compensation; lengthening legislative sessions and/or removing constitutional limitations on the
length of sessions; providing for annual sessions of the legislature
where they were not permissible; reducing the qualifying age for
election to one or both houses of the legislature; making the legislature a continuing body by developing a system of staggered elections; removing or simplifying constitutional requirements as to
legislative procedures; lengthening the terms of legislators, of
members of the lower house to four years, of the upper house even to
six years; requiring all sessions of legislatures and their committees
to be open; and requiring the formulation of a legislative code of
ethics.
Other recommendations would have increased legislative power by
specifically extending it to new areas of concern, such as the protection of the environment, by granting general authorizations
heretofore lacking, or by removing certain areas from the constitution and giving power to act in them to the legislature instead.
A common example of the latter was giving the legislature power to
incorporate, merge, or change local government boundaries and powers.

Executive Reform

The rapid growth of government services expected by the people
after World War II led to a vast increase in the amount of social
legislation that had to be enacted by state legislatures, either on
their own or in response to federal initiatives, and so to similar

increases in administrative activity. Not only was the governor looked to for program leadership, but the executive branch had imposed upon it a tremendous burden of program implementation. In order to accommodate these developments, considerable constitutional change was necessary in most states. The various possibilities before the revision bodies included: reducing the constitutional minimum age for a governor to serve; lengthening the governor's term of office from two to four years, and allowing him to be reelected once where that was prohibited; strengthening the governor's power in state government by enabling him to reorganize the executive branch (subject to some type of legislative veto) and by giving him a reduction or amendatory veto power; allowing him more time to act on a bill after adjournment; giving him increased authority for law enforcement; and providing a procedure for determining gubernatorial disability.

Consideration was also given to providing for the joint election of the governor and the lieutenant governor, providing a shorter ballot by eliminating or lowering the number of elected executive officials designated in the constitution and limiting to two terms in office the remaining constitutional officers; restricting the number of executive departments (somehow twenty seemed to become the magic figure); and abolishing or reorganizing certain boards and agencies provided for in the constitution.

Judicial Reform

Over the years a good deal of evidence had accumulated that state judicial systems were not serving as the agents of justice they were intended to be, and a number of possible alterations to make them more responsive had been proposed. Especially as the rights of minorities came more and more to be asserted, demands for judicial change accumulated. It was a rare convention or commission between 1959 and 1975 that thus did not have before it a variety of propositions for judicial reform. Among those considered were: judicial reorganization and systematization under the Chief Justice of the state's highest court; appointment of judges (rather than their election) according to a variety of schemes, the favorite involving some sort of nominating commission; vesting in the highest state court the power to make rules for state courts (and removal of that power from the legislature); inserting the requirement of judicial retirement at 70 and providing ways of determining judicial inability to serve other than by legislative removal; creating a judicial inquiry board or judicial standards commission to exercise some kind of control over the conduct of judges; and abolishing justice of the peace courts. The New York Convention of 1967 proposed that the state absorb all the costs of the judicial system, so as to relieve local governments of the burden of much of its support.

Changes in Local Government

From the beginning state constitutions have carried provisions

relating to the establishment, powers, and control of local government, in consequence of the holding of Dillon's Rule which makes
local government the creature of the states. A local government article has always been a commonplace in state constitutions. Few
articles required more attention by the decade of the sixties, for
in most cases, local government articles were restrictive in tone,
making it difficult, if not impossible, for local governments to
make the changes required by industrialization and urbanization, the
so-called "home rule" provisions in some constitutions notwithstand-
ing. Indeed, so much negative attention had been paid in most state
constitutions to local government that the local government articles
were often the longest in the document. If the research on state and
local government after the war showed anything, it was the need to
remove the constitutional shackles on effective urban government.
Often this involved nothing more than deleting phrases and sentences
from the local government article; but in many cases it involved
making a positive state commitment. Thus the Rhode Island Convention
of 1964-1965 stipulated in the draft it presented for ratification
by the voters that cities and towns in the state had in effect what
amounts to reserved powers, in that they were presumed to have the
right to exercise any power or perform any function not specifically
denied them in other parts of the proposed constitution or in the
general laws of the state. The Maryland Convention of 1967 came up
with much the same proposal, except that in its recommendation
counties were recognized as the basic units of local government in
the state. The Maryland Convention also recommended that counties
be allowed to exercise only those taxing powers specifically granted
to them by state legislature. Other conventions proposed expanded
self-determination for cities and towns, reorganization of county
government, and authorization for intergovernmental cooperation and
consolidation.

Perhaps the major local government problem in the most populous
states was how to deal with government in metropolitan areas, which
had developed in response to population growth with no regard to existing city and county -- and in some cases, state -- boundary lines.
The Maryland Convention took one approach: to retain existing municipal corporations but to permit counties to create and control new
ones as well as to establish other intracounty governmental units as
needed. Provision was made in the proposed Maryland constitution for
multicounty governmental units created by the legislature, including
intergovernmental authorities and popularly elected representative
regional governments, which might take in any two or more counties.
Other approaches involved a reorganization of county government,
granting more meaningful municipal and/or county home rule, and
authorization for intergovernmental cooperation and consolidation.

Fiscal Changes

State constitutions have obviously always had to deal with the
state's power to tax, borrow, and spend. Bitter experience in the
1800s taught the framers of state constitutions that they must restrict
and limit legislatures in this area, and that lesson remained vivid in

the minds of later revising bodies. Much of the pressure leading to
demands for constitutional change in the sixties came from the need
to remove strings from legislative fiscal powers and to make the states
better able to meet the increasing needs of the urban citizens. It
can be argued that the major cause for the outpouring of federal aid
after 1933 was the constitutional inability of the states to exercise effective fiscal power. Along with the need to enable the
states to meet their own revenue needs and those of their subdivisions
was a good deal of pressure to relieve the tax burden, particularly
on the elderly and the poor. By the beginning of the period under
consideration here, the need to overcome constitutional limitations
on the adequate provision of resources for state government programs
and services had thus become a major concern of all those interested
in state government reform.

A variety of constitutional remedies were considered by the conventions and commissions of the period: relaxing fiscal restrictions
on localities by removing constitutional debt and tax limits, and in
some cases positively expanding local taxing powers; authorizing
legislatures to incorporate lotteries into the state revenue system;
making provision for establishing state debt limits; transferring
responsibility for welfare assistance from counties to states; modi-
fying strict earmarking of revenues from particular sources; establishing more flexible ceilings for issuing general obligation and
revenue bonds; and making it possible to establish a central invest-
ment board for the state. Some changes were recommended in financial
procedures, among them providing for a two-year budgeting and appropriations period and requiring a uniform system of local government accounting. As far as property tax relief went, the Illinois
Convention of 1969-70 was unique in recommending termination of all
personal property taxes by 1979, but other revision bodies recommended putting into effect an equalized state valuation of property
for tax purposes, providing a three-fold classification of property
for tax purposes, setting state maximum percentages of value for
tax assessment, and providing specified exemptions based on age, health,
and income.

Expanding Natural and Civil Rights

Eight of the Revolutionary constitutions had bills of rights and
since then state constitutions have contained, in addition to scattered
protection of rights elsewhere in the document, bills of rights specifically designed to protect the fundamental rights of their citizens
from the actions of state governments, for the Bill of Rights in the
national Constitution applies only to actions by the federal government, and despite the Supreme Court's application of most of those
guarantees to the states through the Fourteenth Amendment, the importance of state restriction on official action remains. In general,
the provisions of these bills parallel those of the first ten amendments to the U.S. Constitution. Too often, a state bill of rights is
not "in harmony with the status of individual rights on the contem-
porary scene. Sometimes...an elaborate bill of rights omits certain

rights, such as the New Hampshire Constitution which does not provide a guarantee for freedom of religion."[28] In some states, thus,
constitutional revisions have been made to the bill of rights in an
effort to meet current problems. In some cases what was needed was
a clearer expression of the constitutional protections for accused
persons and of the rights available to minority groups. In other
cases, the removal of obsolete provisions and consolidation of rights
in one place in the constitution was required. And in still others,
totally new departures were indicated. The Michigan Convention of
1962, for example, established a state civil rights commission to help
secure equal protection of civil rights without dsicrimination, and
the Illinois Convention of 1970 proposed that a healthful environment
be recognized as a citizen's right, to be enforced by giving citizens
the right to sue individuals or organizations that created pollution.

A good deal of attention was necessarily paid to voting in the
constitutional bodies of the period, as the same pressures that finally
forced Congress to pass the Voting Rights Act of 1965 were applied
to the states. Common recommendations were to reduce residence requirements, often from the one year in existing constitutions to 90
days, and (before the 26th Amendment to the U.S. Constitution made
it unnecessary) to lower the voting age from 21 years. In a number
of conventions and commissions, consideration was given to making
special constitutional provisions for presidential primaries. Men-
tion has already been made of recommendations to shorten the ballot
by the reduction of the number of elected executives so as to make
the job of the voter easier.

Constitutional Simplification

Subjected over the years to piecemeal amendment and partial revision, as most state constitutions had been by the early sixties,
and needlessly detailed as most of them were at the outset, by the
beginning of the period being reviewed here, many state constitutions could be compared to "a cluttered, crowded and dimly lighted"
attic that desperately wanted sorting and cleaning out.[29] Virtually
none of the older constitutions was not afflicted with the malady.
Thus even though it is generally recognized that "the Massachusetts
Constitution of 1780 has survived as the oldest constitution in
continuous use in the United States because 85 amendments [had] suc-
cessfully proposed to the electorate" by 1966, and thereby kept the
constitution a viable document,[30] the very addition of those amendments made simplification of the constitutional text imperative.
"Obsolete sections of the Constitution [had] not been deleted in
view of the new amendments.... The new amendments [had] simply been
added to the end of the document rather than being incorporated into
the text." The result was a "generally confusing" document badly in
need of being made "more intelligible." Like many other much amended
constitutions -- The Statesman's Year-Book 1974-1975 reported 324
amendments to the Alabama Constitution of 1901, 212 to the Texas
Constitution of 1876, and 164 to the Nebraska constitution of 1875
(altogether, it reported eleven constitutions with more than 90
amendments each) -- the Massachusetts constitution had become "de-

ficient in its extensive dispersion of material, in its proliferation
of nullified and obsolete provisions and in its cumbersome internal
organization."[31]

In response to this situation, the aim of a good many commissions
and conventions during the period, along with making substantive
changes, was to shorten and simplify the existing constitution. The
new constitution proposed by the Montana Convention of 1971-72, for
example, was a mere 11,200 words in length, about half the length of
the document it was proposed to replace. The draft proposed by the
Rhode Island Convention of 1964-65 was likewise much shorter than the
existing document, was logically organized, and had integrated the
amendments made over the years into the new organization, thus making
that state's basic law at last easy to read. And the proposed constitution submitted in 1966 by the Constitution Revision Assembly in
Kentucky eliminated "a great deal of detail with respect to such
matters as election procedures, local government, and taxation and
finance, as well as much essentially statutory material on corporations, railroads, and commerce."[32]

In some instances, editorial work and simplifications was not carried on across the board. Thus the New York Convention of 1967 proposed a greatly shortened and simplified constitution, but one in
which the "reduction [had been] accomplished...without any appreciable
simplification of the very long and complicated judicial, state finance, local finance, and local government articles."[33]

Miscellaneous

In several conventions and commissions, issues peculiar to particular states dominated or were prominent in discussion. Some
of them may prove to be bellwethers for future revision bodies in
other states. It is not possible to list all the individual issues
raised over the period, but among them were: the need for a constitutional right to work provision; changes in the education article of
the constitution; proposals for specific inclusion in the constitution of conservation and protection of the environment as state re-
sponsibilities; proposals for a constitutional guarantee of the right
of candidates for public office to a fair election; the propriety of
a constitutional requirement of disclosure of election campaign ex-
penditures by candidates for top state offices; and provision for
permanent registration of voters. Special note should be made of the
fairly common proposal emanating from the conventions and commissions
of the period to liberalize the constitutional amendment and revision process itself, often by reducing the majority required to adopt
constitutional amendments, or by removing or lowering the limit on
the number of proposed amendments to the constitution on any one
ballot. These changes are important in that they get at one of the
major causes of constitutional rigidity, the difficulty of initiating
and carrying through desired change.

III

The foregoing discussion of the issues considered by the revision bodies and recommendations made to resolve them may suggest that the conventions and commissions of the period between 1959 and 1975 brought about a virtual revolution in American state government. A great deal was indeed accomplished -- state and local government were generally revivified and redirected, if not in every detail, in many. Conspicuous for the advances made in state government as a result of constitutional revision were Connecticut, Hawaii, and Illinois. And the ideas generated by and expounded in the debates of the conventions and commissions are still very much alive, producing the likelihood that more change yet is in store.

It is impossible to measure precisely the performance of constitutional revision bodies. A great deal would have to be known about the conditions in each state that demanded improvement by constitutional revision before any kind of substantial judgment could be made as to how effective the response was. Moreover, there is an inevitable time lag involved -- in many cases, the impact of a particular constitutional change may not be fully felt for a number of years. And in any case there are no precise instruments available to tell us whether a given imporvement is in fact the result of constitutional change, or of it in combination with other factors, or of other factors alone.

Even so, there is a yardstick against which to measure work in the field of constitutional revision. The October 1967 Report to the National Governor's Conference by the Study Committee on Constitutional Revision and Government Reorganization set forth a series of propositions for a modern, effective state constitution. Those propositions are as follows:

1. The state constitution should express only fundamental law and principle and omit procedural details except, of course, for procedural provisions in the bill of rights;
2. Outmoded, obsolete detail should be removed from the constitution, and material relating to a common subject should be placed in the same article;
3. A constitutional commission composed of persons representing the public as well as government is the best instrument for studying and recommending revisions under (1) and (2) above;
4. Revision of the executive, legislative, and judicial articles should be on the basis of a "whole article" rather than a piecemeal approach;
5. The legislature should be permitted to meet in annual sessions of unlimited length;
6. More authority, fiscal and otherwise, should be granted to local governments, in order to allow Governors and legislatures to concentrate on state problems;
7. The amendment process should be liberalized to allow legislatures to submit more amendments of greater scope and with more frequency; submission of whole articles dealing with the same

subject which would permit more rapid constitutional improvement;

8. One of the most challenging areas of constitutional reform is the fiscal article, which is often a jungle of lengthy and tangled provisions and restrictions; this article should have high priority in revision, and the legislature should be allowed the widest possible range of tax and appropriation alternatives;

9. There should be provision, in addition to legislative option, for placing before the voters at stated intervals the question of whether a constitutional convention shall be called; voters should also have the power, through the initiative process, to call a convention and propose amendments.

When these propositions are matched against the recommendations of the conventions and commissions considered here, it is obvious that the recommendations and proposals of the most of the bodies at work between 1959 and 1975 were squarely in the middle of the ball park. Not every proposition listed there was included in every set of recommendations. The intent of some was only a partial revision, of others to write an entirely new document. It is not easy to compare the products of bodies with such different purposes in mind. Even do, it is possible to conclude from reviewing the nine statements that American states have gone a long way toward modernizing the bases of their governments since 1959, continuing a trend begun well before that. Whether constitutional modernization also has prepared the states to meet the future more effectively remains to be seen. It probably is in vain to hope to be able to foresee what kinds of economic, social, and cultural changes will require state action in the future and, therefore, vain to hope that the constitutional changes in the sixties and seventies will be enough for the rest of time. Whenever the next round of revision comes about, however, it will have the great advantage of being able to build on a solid foundation of experience, both in how to mount and carry on the revision process itself and in developing a suitable range of substantive alternatives to consider. In fact, the raw material for the next round of revision may well be found in the pages of the items listed in the bibliography that follows this essay.

However diligently and effectively the conventions and commissions worked at their tasks of revision, their recommendations were not always received enthusiastically by the voters. The constitutions offered by revision bodies in New York, Maryland, Rhode Island, and New Mexico, for example, were turned down at the ballot bax. Defeat of a proposed constitution has not necessarily meant rejection by the people, however. For one thing, votes in constitutional referenda are traditionally small, tending to reflect the "antis" on one or two particular points rather than the general public attitude toward the issues involved. The voter turnout in the Rhode Island constitutional referendum on the constitution proposed by the 1968-1969 convention was a mere 19 percent. Looming large among those who did not vote were opponents of the proposed state lottery. Some of the courses for rejection have been identified, for example, annoyance at the extra burden placed upon the voters, a vague fear that a new constitution and the strengthened government it would bring about, would mean higher taxes; poor timing; too little time available between the end of the convention and the holding of the referendum; and the lack of an effective program of public information. (It is ironical that the Maryland Convention of 1967 carefully provided for "a committee of public information with staff and officers to carry out a program of public information on the proposed constitution," once it was completed,[34] yet it was one of the constitutions that went down in defeat!) Indeed, among the lessons learned by the revision exercise of the sixties was that proposals fare better with the public when they are presented as separate entities rather than as a single package.

Nor was every product of a convention or commission wholly meritorious. Thus one comment on the proposed new Florida Constitution of 1968 (which incidentally was adopted by the voters) was to the effect that several vitally important subjects were completely omitted, that restrictions were placed on local government which would "make its adequacy questionable...in the next few years," and that generally "it simply pulled the old existing provisions together in a somewhat reorganized fashion, improved and corrected the general composition and syntax to some extent, and added very little new material or powers." Indeed, that comment went on, "One cannot but conclude that if Florida earlier needed a new state constitution...it still [stood] in need of one after the convention had adjourned in 1968."[35]

Looking ahead, two trends seem to be developing: (1) a greater reliance on legislative amendment than on changes proposed by constitutional commissions and constitutional conventions (at least, Albert L. Sturm reported in 1974 that "compared with the previous two biennia, the States placed less emphasis on general revision by constitutional conventions and constitutional commissions and more on proposals by the Legislatures"[36]), due in large part to the poor reception the proposals of so many conventions and commissions received from the voters; (2) a slackening of the pace of reform activity in the rest of the seventies, as fewer states than ever before stand in need of extensive constitutional reform. It is likely, indeed, that the period from 1959-1975 will remain for a long time the most productive period of constitutional change since the first round of revision in the 1820s.

In the final analysis, it remains to be said, a new or revised constitution in and of itself may offer little to the solution of a state's problems. "Constitutions, like all legal documents, can have but little permanent shape and effect beyond the good faith and ability of those called upon to put them into practice [and] the willingness of the governed to accept them as binding political instruments and to abide by their provisions as authoritatively expounded by those who have the legal power of final exposition."[37] As one observer in Texas noted, "the nature of the Constitution... is only incidental to whether Texas has an honest, efficient, principled government. The caliber of the men who guide the state's affairs determines the type of government Texas has. The most ideal constitution will be of aid to honest public officials, but will have little bearing on the activities of unscrupulous ones. Until each individual voter demonstrates a willingness to accept the never-ending responsibility of selecting trustworthy public servants, public morality, idealism, and self-restraint will often be ignored by those who seek to obtain public office. The choice seems not to lie between a superb modern constitution and an outmoded, over-amended, antiquated document, but between a disinterested citizenry and a citizenry that accepts the duties as well as the privileges of a democratic form of government."[38] Even so, the help a modern constitution can be to honest public servants can be great, and so constitutional revision remains a continuing necessity if American government is to meet the mounting challenges of an uncertain future.

NOTES

1. See Charles R. Adrian, "Trends in State Constitutions." Harvard Journal on Legislation 5: (March 1968), 311-341.

2. Albert L. Sturm, "State Constitutions and Constitutional Revision. 1967-1969," The Book of the States 1970-1971 (Lexington, Ky., 1972), p. 7. See below.

3. W. Brook Graves, "State Constitutions and Constitutional Revision, 1963-1965," The Book of the States 1966-1967 (Chicago, 1968), pp. 6-7.

4. Sturm, "State Constitutions and Constitutional Revision, 1970-1971," The Book of the States 1972-73 (Lexington, Ky., 1972), p. 7.

5. Sturm, "1967-1969," p. 6.

6. See especially the following National Municipal League publications: Gordon E. Baker, State Constitutions: Reapportionment (New York, 1960). John P. Wheeler, Jr., ed., Salient Issues of Constitutional Revision (New York, 1961) and The Constitutional Convention: A Manual on Its Planning, Organization and Operation (New York, 1961). Robert B. Dishman, The Shape of the Document (New York, 1960). Balfour J. Halevy with Libby H. Guth, A Selective Bibliography on State Constitutional Revision (New York, 1963). State Constitutional Studies. 10 vols. in two series (New York, 1960-65) Model State Constitution. 6th ed. (New York, 1963).

7. E.g., League of Women Voters of the United States, Inventory of Work on State Constitutional Revision by State Leagues of Women Voters (Washington, 1960).

8. E.g., Terry Sanford, Storm Over the States (New York, 1967).

9. Graves, "1963-1965," p. 3.

10. John E. Bebout, "State Constitutions and Constitutional Revision, 1965-1967," The Book of the States 1968-1969 (Chicago, 1969), p. 3.

11. Sturm, "1967-1969," p. 3.

12. E.g., Committee for Economic Development, <u>Modernizing State Gov-</u><u>ernment</u> (New York, 1967) and <u>Modernizing Local Government</u> (New York, 1966); National Governors' Conference, <u>The States and Urban</u> <u>Problems</u> (Washington, 1967); Public Administration Service, <u>Con-</u><u>stitutional Studies</u>, 3 vols. (Chicago, 1955); and various issues of <u>State Government</u>, the journal of the Council of State Govern- ments, during the sixties.

13. Sturm, "1967-1969," p. 3.

14. Bebout, "1965-1967," p. 6.

15. Sturm, "State Constitutions and Constitutional Revision, 1972- 1973," <u>The Book of the States 1974-1975</u> (Lexington, Ky., 1974), p. 8.

16. Graves, "1963-1965," p. 7.

17. Bebout, "1965-1967," p. 8.

18. Graves, "1963-1965," p. 5.

19. Sturm, "1970-1971," p. 14.

20. The wisdom of such a provision in terms of providing an appropri- ate climate for discussion at the convention is borne out by the New York Convention of 1967, the enabling act of which did not so specify, with the result that "the convention was conducted more or less in the spirit of party battles," which in a conven- tion of 186 members may have been enough to doom its efforts from the start. (Bebout, "1965-67," p. 6.)

21. Sturm, "1967-1969," p. 13.

22. John A. Straayer, <u>American State and Local Government</u> (Columbus, Ohio, 1973), p. 60.

23. Straayer, p. 60.

24. <u>National Municipal Review</u>, October 1937, p. 465.

25. These and the quoted portions of items number 2-8 are from Albert L. Sturm, <u>Public Affairs</u> (the publication of the Govern- mental Research Bureau, University of South Dakota, August 15, 1968, p. 2.

26. Graves, "1962-1965," p. 3.

27. Sturm, "1970-1971," p. 7.

28. John C. Buechner, <u>State Government in the Twentieth Century</u> (Boston, 1967), p. 65.

29. The words of an unnamed former governor of California, quoted in Graves, "1963-1965," p. 6.

30. In November 1966, Massachusetts voters approved "four general amendments that added up to more extensive constitutional revision than has resulted from limited conventions in some states or from efforts of constitutional revision commissions in some others." (Bebout, "1965-1967," p. 4.)

31. Robert A. Shanley, The Problem of Simplifying the Massachusetts Constitution (Amherst, Mass., 1966), pp. 3, 39.

32. Bebout, "1965-1967," p. 11.

33. Bebout, "1965-1967," p. 6.

34. Bebout, "1965-1969," p. 9.

35. Manning J. Dauer, Clement H. Donovan, and Gladys M. Kammerer, Should Florida Adopt the Proposed 1968 Constitution? An Analysis (Gainesville, Fla., 1968), pp. 3-4.

36. Sturm, "1972-1973," p. 3.

37. Committee to Cooperate with the International Commission of Jurists Section on International and Comparative Law, The Rule of Law in the United States (New York, 1958), p. 50.

38. Wilbourn E. Benton, quoted in A. J. Thomas, Jr., and Ann Van Wynen Thomas, "The Texas Constitution of 1876," Texas Law Review, Special Issue on Constitutional Revision in Texas (October 1957), 918.

STATE CONSTITUTIONAL CONVENTIONS

Arkansas

[Ar 14]
Arkansas. Constitution.
    Constitution of the State of Arkansas with all amend-
ments, September 1963. [Little Rock]. Kelly Bryant,
Secretary of State [1963].
    116 p.

[Ar 15]
Arkansas. Constitutional Revision Study Commission.
    Revising the Arkansas Constitution; a report to the
Honorable Winthrop Rockefeller, Governor of the State of
Arkansas and Members of the Sixty-sixth General Assembly
of the State of Arkansas. Little Rock, 1968.
    ix, 152 p.

[Ar 16]
Arkansas. Constitutional Convention, 1969.
    Delegate Proposals. [Little Rock] 1969.
    v.p.

[Ar 17]
Arkansas. Constitutional Convention, 1969.
    Committee Proposals. [Little Rock] 1969.
    v.p.

[Ar 18]
Arkansas. Constitutional Convention, 1969.
    Proposed Arkansas Constitution of 1970, with Comments.
A Report to the People of Arkansas by the Seventh Arkansas
Constitutional Convention. February 10, 1970. Little Rock,
Arkansas.
    xv, 101 p.

[Ar 19]
Arkansas. Secretary of State.
    Constitution of the State of Arkansas with all Amend-
ments. Published by Kelly Bryant, Secretary of State
[Little Rock] January 1975.
    130 p.

Connecticut

[Ct 15]
Connecticut. House of Representatives.
    File No. 1--An Act Establishing A Constitutional Conven-
tion. Hartford, 1964.
    8 p.

[Ct 16]
Connecticut. Constitutional Convention, 1965. Planning
    Commission.
    Proceedings of the Planning Commission of the Constitu-
tional Convention, May 5-June 30, 1965. Public Hearings,
May 24, 1965. [Hartford], 1965.
    495 p.

[Ct 17]
Connecticut. Constitutional Convention, 1965.
    Constitutional Convention Research Reports, September
1965. [Hartford], 1965.
    v.p.

[Ct 18]
Connecticut. Constitutional Convention, 1965.
    Resolutions of the 1965 Constitutional Convention of
Connecticut, Numbers 1-259. [Hartford], 1965.
    v.p.

[Ct 19]
Connecticut. Constitutional Convention, 1965.
    Constitutional Resolutions Committee Hearings, Rules
Committee Hearings, July 1-October 28, 1965. [Hartford], 1965.
    v.p.

[Ct 20]
Connecticut. Constitutional Convention, 1965.
    Appendix (to resolutions) Numbers 1-23. [Hartford], 1965.
    v.p.

[Ct 21]
Connecticut. Constitutional Convention, 1965.
    File Numbers 2, 3, 7, 9, 11, 13, 16, 19 & 20. [Hartford],
1965.
    v.p.

[Ct 22]
Connecticut. Constitutional Convention, 1965.
    Reapportionment Committee Hearings, July 1-October 28,
1965. [Hartford], 1965.
    202 p.

[Ct 23]
Connecticut. Constitutional Convention, 1965.
    Constitutional Convention Record Index by Subject Matter,
August 1965. [Hartford], 1965.
    24 p.

[Ct 24]
Connecticut. Constitutional Convention, 1965.
    Proceedings of the 1965 Constitutional Convention of Con-
necticut, July 1-October 28, 1965. [Hartford], 1965.
    3 v.

[Ct 25]
Connecticut. Constitutional Convention, 1965.
    Public Hearings and Public Meetings of the 1965 Consti-
tutional Convention of Connecticut. [Hartford], 1965.
    369 p.

[Ct 26]
Connecticut. Constitutional Convention, 1965.
    Journal of the 1965 Constitutional Convention of the
State of Connecticut. Hartford, 1965.
    240 p.

[Ct 27]
Connecticut. Constitutional Convention, 1965.
    Proposed Revised Constitution for the State with Marginal
Notes. Hartford, 1966.
    22 p.

[Ct 28]
Connecticut. Constitutional Convention, 1965.
    Resume of Proposals Passed by the Constitutional Conven-
tion of 1965. [Hartford, 1966.]
    6 p.

[Ct 29]
Connecticut. Constitutional Convention, 1965.
    Analysis of Expenditures as Prepared by Auditors of
Public Accounts. Hartford, 1966.
    1 p.

[Ct 30]
Connecticut. Constitution.
    Constitution of the State of Connecticut and Historical
Antecedents. Office of the Secretary of State. [Hartford],
1966.
    49 p.

Florida

[Fl 23]
Florida. Constitution.
Constitution of the State of Florida, Adopted by the
Convention of 1885 (as Amended). Distributed by Tom Adams,
Secretary of State. [Tallahassee], 1967.
4,001-4,085 p.

[Fl 24]
Florida. Constitutional Revision Commission.
Commission Minutes, Committee Minutes and Proposals:
January 1966-June 1966. Tallahassee, [1966].
347 l.

[Fl 25]
Florida. Legislature.
Draft of Proposed 1968 Constitution Submitted by the Legislature to the Voters for Ratification at the General Election of November 5, 1968. [Tallahassee], 1968.
27 p.

[Fl 26]
Florida. Constitution.
Constitution of the State of Florida, as Amended in 1968.
Distributed by Tom Adams, Secretary of State. [Tallahassee],
1969.
56 p.

Hawaii

[Ha 7]
Hawaii. Legislature.
  Act 280, Session Laws of the State of Hawaii, 1965.
  2 p.   (Enabling Legislation)

[Ha 8]
Hawaii. Constitution.
  The Constitution of the State of Hawaii, as Amended and
in Force, May 1, 1966. Honolulu, Archives Division, Department of Accounting and General Services, 1966.
  30 p.

[Ha 9]
Hawaii. Legislature.
  Act 222, Session Laws of the State of Hawaii, 1967.
  4 p.   (Enabling Legislation)

[Ha 10-26]
Hawaii. Legislative Reference Bureau.
  Hawaii Constitutional Convention Studies. Honolulu,
[1968].
  17 v.

[Ha 10]
Hawaii. Legislative Reference Bureau.
  Constitutional Convention Study #1--Constitutional Convention Organization Procedures, by Annette Miyagi.
  106 p.

[Ha 11]
Hawaii. Legislative Reference Bureau.
  Constitutional Convention Study #2--Introduction and
Article Summaries.
  179 p.

[Ha 12]
Hawaii. Legislative Reference Bureau.
  Constitutional Convention Study #3--Article 1: Bill of
Rights by, Wayne K. Minami and Judy E. Stalling.
  201 p.

[Ha 13]
Hawaii. Legislative Reference Bureau.
  Constitutional Convention Study #4--Article 2: Suffrage
and Elections, by Judy E. Stalling.
  86 p.

[Ha 14]
Hawaii. Legislative Reference Bureau.
    Constitutional Convention Study #5--Article 3:   The Leg-
islature, Part 1 by, Judy E. Stalling.
    99 p.

[Ha 15]
Hawaii. Legislative Reference Bureau.
    Constitutional Convention Study #6--Article 3:   The Leg-
islature, Part 2 (Apportionment Provisions), by Bertram Kan-
bara, Yokio Naito, and Patricia Snyder.
    19 p.

[Ha 16]
Hawaii. Legislative Reference Bureau.
    Constitutional Convention Study #7--Article 4:   The Ex-
ecutive, by Marie E. Gillespie [and others].
    139 p.

[Ha 17]
Hawaii. Legislative Reference Bureau.
    Constitutional Convention Study #8--Article 5:   The Ju-
diciary, by Wayne K. Minami.
    104 p.

[Ha 18]
Hawaii. Legislative Reference Bureau.
    Constitutional Convention Study #9--Article 6:   Taxation
and Finance, by Newton N. S. Sue and Thomas W. Wong.
    122 p.

[Ha 19]
Hawaii. Legislative Reference Bureau.
    Constitutional Convention Study #10--Article 7:   Local
Government by Judy E. Stalling.
    71 p.

[Ha 20]
Hawaii. Legislative Reference Bureau.
    Constitutional Convention Study #11--Article 8:   Public
Health and Welfare, by Richard J. Richardson.
    41 p.

[Ha 21]
Hawaii. Legislative Reference Bureau.
    Constitutional Convention Study #12--Article 9:   Educa-
tion, Part 1 (Public Education), by Millicent Y. H. Kim.
    114 p.

[Ha 22]
Hawaii. Legislative Reference Bureau.
    Constitutional Convention Study #13--Article 9:   Educa-
tion, Part 2 (Higher Education), by Millicent Y. H. Kim.
    56 p.

[Ha 23]
Hawaii. Legislative Reference Bureau.
Constitutional Convention Study #14--Article 10: Conservation and Development of Resources, by Charles Mark; Article 11: Hawaiian Home   nds, by Patricia Snyder.
110 p.

[Ha 24]
Hawaii. Legislative Reference Bureau.
Constitutional Convention Study #15--Article 12: Organization, Collective Bargaining, by Harold S. Roberts.
122 p.

[Ha 25]
Hawaii. Legislative Reference Bureau.
Constitutional Convention Study #16--Article 13: State Boundaries, Capital, Flag, by Sonia A. Faust and Mildred Lim; Article 14: General and Miscellaneous Provisions, by Millicent Y. H. Kim; Article 16: Schedule, by Harriete Joesting.
136 p.

[Ha 26]
Hawaii. Legislative Reference Bureau.
Constitutional Convention Study #17--Article 15: Revision and Amendment, by Judy E. Stalling.
63 p.

[Ha 27A-B]
Hawaii. Constitutional Convention, 1968.
Proceedings of the Constitutional Convention of the State of Hawaii of 1968. Published under the supervision of the Administrator of the Convention, Honolulu, 197-.
2 v.

[Ha 27A]
Hawaii. Constitutional Convention, 1968.
Proceedings of the Constitutional Convention of the State, Volume 1--Journal and Documents. 1973.
xxiii, 524 p.

[Ha 27B]
Hawaii. Constitutional Convention, 1968.
Proceedings of the Constitutional Convention of the State, Volume 2--Committee of the Whole Debates. 1972.
xii, 554 p.

[Ha 28]
Hawaii. Constitution.
The Constitution of the State of Hawaii, as Amended by the Constitutional Convention, 1968, and Adopted by the Electorate on November 5, 1968. Honolulu, Archives Division, Department of Accounting and General Services, 1969.
32 p.

Illinois

[Il 32]
Illinois. Constitution.
   Constitution of the State of Illinois. Adopted May 3,
1870. Issued by Paul Powell, Secretary of State [Spring-
field, 1966.]
   90 p.

   "Constitution of the United States: pp 70-80."
   "The Constitution of Illinois as amended throuqh 1964,
and the Constitution of the United States as amended with
Amendment XXIV."

[Il 33]
Illinois. Constitution Study Commission.
   Report of the Constitution Study Commission created
by the 74th General Assembly. [Springfield], 1967.
   23 p.

[Il 34]
Illinois. Constitution Study Commission.
   Preparing for the Illinois Constitutional Convention,
Report of the Constitution Study Commission. [Springfield],
June, 1969.
   38 p.

   "This report is the final report of the Constitution
Study Commission to the Governor and the members of the 76th
General Assembly."

[Il 35]
Illinois. Constitution Study Commission.
   Launching the Sixth Illinois Constitutional Convention:
The Last Giant Step! Report of the Constitution Study Commission created by the 76th General Assembly. [Springfield,
1970.]
   36 p.

[Il 36]
Illinois. Constitutional Convention, 1969-1970.
   Members: Illinois Constitutional Convention, 1969-1970.
Issued by Paul Powell, Secretary of State. [Springfield,
Illinois Allied Printing, 1969.]
   122 p.   ports.

[Il 37]
Illinois. Constitution Research Group.
   Con-con: Issues for the Illinois Constitutional Convention, Papers. Samuel K. Gove, director. Victoria Ranney, editor. Urbana, University of Illinois Press [1970].
   xi, 512 p.

   "A collection of papers prepared for the Illinois convention, at the request of the Governor, on issues which were to face the convention."

[Il 38A-C]
Illinois. Constitutional Convention, 1969-1970.
   Record of Proceedings, Sixth Illinois Constitutional Convention. [Springfield, Secretary of State, 1972.]
   7 v.

[Il 38A]
Illinois. Constitutional Convention, 1969-1970.
   Record of Proceedings--Daily Journals, December 8, 1969-September 3, 1970.
   921 p.

[Il 38B]
Illinois. Constitutional Convention, 1969-1970.
   Record of Proceedings--Verbatim Transcripts, December 8, 1969-September 3, 1970.
   4 v.

[Il 38C]
Illinois. Constitutional Convention, 1969-1970.
   Record of Proceedings--Committee Proposals and Member Proposals, December 8, 1969-September 3, 1970.
   2 v.

[Il 39]
Fishbane, Joyce D.
   Politics of the Purse: Revenue and Finance in the Sixth Illinois Constitutional Convention, [by] Joyce D. Fishbane and Glenn W. Fisher. Studies in Illinois Constitution Making. Urbana, published for the Institute of Government and Public Affairs by the University of Illinois Press, [1974].
   xv, 199 p.

[Il 40]
Illinois. Constitution.
   Constitution of the State of Illinois and of the United States, Springfield, 1970.
   90 p.

Louisiana

[La 33]
Public Affairs Research Council of Louisiana, Inc.
   A Procedure for Revising Louisiana's Constitution. Baton Rouge, 1969.
      vii, 104 p.

[La 34]
Public Affairs Research Council of Louisiana, Inc.
   Constitutional Convention 1973--A Preview. Baton Rouge, 1972.
      29 p.

[La 35]
Louisiana. Constitutional Convention, 1973-1974.
   Official Journal of the Proceedings of the Constitutional Convention of 1973 of the State of Louisiana, held in accordance with Act 2 of the 1972 Regular Session of the Legislature as amended, January 5, 1973-January 19, 1974. Baton Rouge, 1974.
      2 volumes

[La 36]
Louisiana. Constitutional Convention, 1973-1974.
   Proposed Constitution of the State of Louisiana. Baton Rouge, 1974.
      iii, 47 p. [6 leaves]

[La 37]
Public Affairs Research Council of Louisiana, Inc.
   PAR's Voter's Guide to the 1974 Proposed Constitution. Baton Rouge, 1974.
      44 p.

Maryland

[Md 21–28]
Maryland. Constitutional Convention Commission.
    [Committee reports...Annapolis, 1965-1967.]
    8 v.

[Md 21]
Maryland. Constitutional Convention Commission.
    Committee on Convention Procedures. Reports, 1st-8th,
and Proposed Standing Rules.
    123 p.

[Md 22]
Maryland. Constitutional Convention Commission.
    Committee on the Judiciary Department. Reports, 1st-8th
(Final).
    220 p.

[Md 23]
Maryland. Constitutional Convention Commission.
    Committee on Legislative Department. Reports, 1st-9th
(Final).
    122 p.

[Md 24]
Maryland. Constitutional Convention Commission.
    Committee on Miscellaneous Provisions. Reports, Initial-
8th.
    89 p.

[Md 25]
Maryland. Constitutional Convention Commission.
    Committee on Political Subdivisions and Local Legislation.
Reports, 1st (Rev.)-8th (Final).
    158 p.

[Md 26]
Maryland. Constitutional Convention Commission.
    Committee on State Finance and Taxation. Reports, 1st-
3rd.
    101 p.

[Md 27]
Maryland. Constitutional Convention Commission.
    Committee on the Declaration of Rights and Elective
Franchise. Reports, 1st-9th.
    98 p.

[Md 28]
Maryland. Constitutional Convention Commission.
Committee on Executive Department. Reports 1st (Rev.)_
8th, and meeting of the Committee on the Executive Department with Governor J. M. Tawes...February 24, 1966. Baltimore, Maryland.
191 p.

[Md 29A-29M]
Maryland. Constitutional Convention Commission.
[Constitutional Convention Commission Proceedings. H.
Vernon Eney, Chairman. Baltimore, 1966.]
15 v.

[Md 29A]
Maryland. Constitutional Convention Commission.
Index and Proceedings of the Commission, June 20, July
17, 1966.
273 p.

[Md 29B]
Maryland. Constitutional Convention Commission.
Proceedings of the Commission, July 17-18, 1966.
468 p.

[Md 29C]
Maryland. Constitutional Convention Commission.
Proceedings of the Commission, August 21-22, 1966.
602 p.

[Md 29D]
Maryland. Constitutional Convention Commission.
Proceedings of the Commission, September 18-19, 1966.
428 p.

[Md 29E]
Maryland. Constitutional Convention Commission.
Proceedings of the Commission, September 19-20, 1966.
461 p.

[Md 29F]
Maryland. Constitutional Convention Commission.
Proceedings of the Commission, October 14, 1966.
389 p.

[Md 29G]
Maryland. Constitutional Convention Commission.
Proceedings of the Commission, October 15-16, 1966.
432 p.

[Md 29H]
Maryland. Constitutional Convention Commission.
Proceedings of the Commission, October 24, 1966.
366 p.

[Md 29I]
Maryland. Constitutional Convention Commission
Proceedings of the Commission, October 25, 1966.
322 p.

[Md 29J]
Maryland. Constitutional Convention Commission.
Proceedings of the Commission, November 21, 1966.
415 p.

[Md 29K]
Maryland. Constitutional Convention Commission.
Proceedings of the Commission, December 3, December 19,
1966.
391 p.

[Md 29L]
Maryland. Constitutional Convention Commission.
Conference on Metropolitan Problems at Goucher College,
December 9-10, 1966.
408 p.

[Md 29M]
Maryland. Constitutional Convention Commission.
Committee Hearings of the Commission.
1524 p.

[Md 30]
Maryland. Constitutional Convention Commission.
Report of the Commission on the Constitutional Convention
Enabling Act, January 16, 1967. Baltimore, 1967.
v, 36 p.

[Md 31]
Maryland. State Law Department.
Opinion of the Attorney General, Francis B. Burch on the
eligibility of members of the General Assembly to serve as
delegates to the Constitutional Convention, January 26,
1967. [Baltimore, 1967.]
10 p.

[Md 32]
Maryland. Constitutional Convention Commission.
Interim eport of the Commission to His Excellency, Spiro
T. Agnew, Governor of Maryland and to The Honorable, The General Assembly of Maryland, May 26, 1967. [Annapolis, Published by the State of Maryland for the Constitutional Convention Commission, 1967.]
x, 219 p.

[Md 33]
Maryland. Constitutional Convention Commission.
Report to His Excellency, Spiro T. Agnew, The Honorable,
The General Assembly of Maryland, the Delegates to the Con-
stitutional Convention of Maryland and to the People of
Maryland, August 25, 1967. [Annapolis, 1967.]
xxi, 594 p. illus.

[Md 34–49]
Maryland. Constitutional Convention, 1967–1968.
[Committee on Daily Calendar, Agenda and Reports; Delegate Proposals; Motions and Resolutions; Proposed Constitutions. Annapolis, 1967.]
20 v.

[Md 34]
Maryland. Constitutional Convention, 1967–1968.
Committee on Daily Calendar and Agenda. Daily Calendar and Agenda and Report, C&A-1.
26 p.

[Md 35]
Maryland. Constitutional Convention, 1967–1968.
Committee on Executive Branch. Reports, EB-1 to EB-2.
202 p.

[Md 36]
Maryland. Constitutional Convention, 1967–1968.
Committee on General Provisions. Reports, GP-1 to GP-13.
282 p.

[Md 37]
Maryland. Constitutional Convention, 1967–1968.
Committee on Judicial Branch. Reports, JB-1 to JB-2.
187 p.

[Md 38]
Maryland. Constitutional Convention, 1967–1968.
Committee on Local Government. Report, LG-1.
79 p.

[Md 39]
Maryland. Constitutional Convention, 1967–1968.
Committee on Personal Rights and Preamble. Reports, R&P-1 to R&P-2.
230 p.

[Md 40]
Maryland. Constitutional Convention, 1967–1968.
Committee on Rules, Credentials and Convention Budget. Reports, R&C-1 to R&C-16.
173 p.

[Md 41]
Maryland. Constitutional Convention, 1967–1968.
Committee on State Finance and Taxation. Reports, SF-1 to SF-5.
96 p.

[Md 42]
Maryland. Constitutional Convention, 1967–1968.
Committee on Style, Drafting and Arrangement. Reports, S&D-1 to S&D-18.
570 p.

[Md 43]
Maryland. Constitutional Convention, 1967-1968.
   Committee on Suffrage and Elections. Reports, S&E-1 to
S&E-2.
   134 p.

[Md 44]
Maryland. Constitutional Convention, 1967-1968.
   Committee on Legislative Branch. Reports, LB-1 to LB-3.
   206 p.

[Md 45]
Maryland. Constitutional Convention, 1967-1968.
   Committee of the Whole. Reports, Numbers 1-33.
   114 p.

[Md 46]
Maryland. Constitutional Convention, 1967-1968.
   Select Committees. Reports.
   6 p.

[Md 47]
Maryland. Constitutional Convention, 1967-1968.
   Delegate Proposals. Numbers 1-445.
   846 p.

[Md 48]
Maryland. Constitutional Convention, 1967-1968.
   Motions and Resolutions.
   123 p.

[Md 49]
Maryland. Constitutional Convention, 1967-1968.
   Proposed Constitutions.
   134 p.

[Md 50A-50p]
Maryland. Constitutional Convention, 1967-1968.
   Constitutional Convention of the State of Maryland [Pro-
ceedings]. H. Vernon Eney, president. Reported by C. J.
Hunt [Annapolis?] 1967-1968.
   42 v.

[Md 50A]
Maryland. Constitutional Convention, 1967-1968.
   Proceedings of the Constitutional Convention of the
State, September 12-22, 1967.
   368 p.

[Md 50B]
Maryland. Constitutional Convention, 1967-1968.
   Proceedings of the Constitutional Convention of the
State, September 25-October 5, 1967.
   363 p.

[Md 50C]
Maryland. Constitutional Convention, 1967-1968.
  Proceedings of the Constitutional Convention of the
State, October 6-26, 1967.
  378 p.

[Md 50D]
Maryland. Constitutional Convention, 1967-1968.
  Proceedings of the Constitutional Convention of the
State, October 30-November 6, 1967.
  381 p.

[Md 50
Maryland. Constitutional Convention, 1967-1968.
  Proceedings of the Constitutional Convention of the
State, November 7-8, 1967.
  526 p.

[Md 50F]
Maryland. Constitutional Convention, 1967-1968.
  Proceedings of the Constitutional Convention of the
State, November 9, 1967.
  298 p.

[Md 50G]
Maryland. Constitutional Convention, 1967-1968.
  Proceedings of the Constitutional Convention of the
State, November 10, 1967.
  304 p.

[Md 50Ga]
Maryland. Constitutional Convention, 1967-1968.
  Proceedings of the Constitutional Convention of the
State, November 13, 1967.
  272 p.

[Md 50H]
Maryland. Constitutional Convention, 1967-1968.
  Proceedings of the Constitutional Convention of the
State, November 14, 1967.
  312 p.

[Md 50I]
Maryland. Constitutional Convention, 1967-1968.
  Proceedings of the Constitutional Convention of the
State, November 15, 1967.
  299 p.

[Md 50J]
Maryland. Constitutional Convention, 1967-1968.
  Proceedings of the Constitutional Convention of the
State, November 16, 1967.
  306 p.

[Md 50K]
Maryland. Constitutional Convention, 1967-1968.
   Proceedings of the Constitutional Convention of the
State, November 17, 1967.
   266 p.

[Md 50L]
Maryland. Constitutional Convention, 1967-1968.
   Proceedings of the Constitutional Convention of the
State, November 20, 1967.
   298 p.

[Md 50M]
Maryland. Constitutional Convention, 1967-1968.
   Proceedings of the Constitutional Convention of the
State, November 21, 1967.
   270 p.

[Md 50N]
Maryland. Constitutional Convention, 1967-1968.
   Proceedings of the Constitutional Convention of the
State, November 22, 1967.
   269 p.

[Md 50Ø]
Maryland. Constitutional Convention, 1967-1968.
   Proceedings of the Constitutional Convention of the
State, November 27, 1967.
   292 p.

[Md 50P]
Maryland. Constitutional Convention, 1967-1968.
   Proceedings of the Constitutional Convention of the
State, November 28, 1967.
   244 p.

[Md 50Q]
Maryland. Constitutional Convention, 1967-1968.
   Proceedings of the Constitutional Convention of the
State, November 29, 1967.
   382 p.

[Md 50R]
Maryland. Constitutional Convention, 1967-1968.
   Proceedings of the Constitutional Convention of the
State, November 30, 1967.
   269 p.

[Md 50S]
Maryland. Constitutional Convention, 1967-1968.
   Proceedings of the Constitutional Convention of the
State, December 1, 1967.
   431 p.

[Md 50T]
Maryland. Constitutional Convention, 1967-1968.
   Proceedings of the Constitutional Convention of the
State, December 2, 1967.
   249 p.

[Md 50U]
Maryland. Constitutional Convention, 1967-1968.
   Proceedings of the Constitutional Convention of the
State, December 4, 1967.
   309 p.

[Md 50V]
Maryland. Constitutional Convention, 1967-1968.
   Proceedings of the Constitutional Convention of the
State, December 5, 1967.
   287 p.

[Md 50W]
Maryland. Constitutional Convention, 1967-1968.
   Proceedings of the Constitutional Convention of the
State, December 6, 1967.
   423 p.

[Md 50X]
Maryland. Constitutional Convention, 1967-1968.
   Proceedings of the Constitutional Convention of the
State, December 7, 1967.
   303 p.

[Md 50Y]
Maryland. Constitutional Convention, 1967-1968.
   Proceedings of the Constitutional Convention of the
State, December 8, 1967.
   310 p.

[Md 50Z]
Maryland. Constitutional Convention, 1967-1968.
   Proceedings of the Constitutional Convention of the
State, December 9, 1967.
   317 p.

[Md 50a]
Maryland. Constitutional Convention, 1967-1968.
   Proceedings of the Constitutional Convention of the
State, December 11, 1967.
   276 p.

[Md 50b]
Maryland. Constitutional Convention, 1967-1968.
   Proceedings of the Constitutional Convention of the
State, December 12, 1967.
   307 p.

[Md 50c]
Maryland. Constitutional Convention, 1967-1968.
   Proceedings of the Constitutional Convention of the
State, December 13, 1967.
   454 p.

[Md 50d]
Maryland. Constitutional Convention, 1967-1968.
   Proceedings of the Constitutional Convention of the
State, December 14, 1967.
   350 p.

[Md 50e]
Maryland. Constitutional Convention, 1967-1968.
   Proceedings of the Constitutional Convention of the
State, December 15, 1967.
   380 p.

[Md 50f]
Maryland. Constitutional Convention, 1967-1968.
   Proceedings of the Constitutional Convention of the
State, December 19, 1967.
   310 p.

[Md 50g]
Maryland. Constitutional Convention, 1967-1968.
   Proceedings of the Constitutional Convention of the
State, December 20-21, 1967.
   453 p.

[Md 50h]
Maryland. Constitutional Convention, 1967-1968.
   Proceedings of the Constitutional Convention of the
State, December 27, 1967.
   231 p.

[Md 50i]
Maryland. Constitutional Convention, 1967-1968.
   Proceedings of the Constitutional Convention of the
State, December 28, 1967.
   282 p.

[Md 50j]
Maryland. Constitutional Convention, 1967-1968.
   Proceedings of the Constitutional Convention of the
State, December 29, 1967.
   380 p.

[Md 50k]
Maryland. Constitutional Convention, 1967-1968.
   Proceedings of the Constitutional Convention of the
State, December 30, 1967.
   206 p.

[Md 501]
Maryland. Constitutional Convention, 1967-1968.
   Proceedings of the Constitutional Convention of the
State, January 2, 1968.
   380 p.

[Md 50m]
Maryland. Constitutional Convention, 1967-1968.
   Proceedings of the Constitutional Convention of the
State, January 3, 1968.
   372 p.

[Md 50n]
Maryland. Constitutional Convention, 1967-1968.
   Proceedings of the Constitutional Convention of the
State, January 4, 1968.
   398 p.

[Md 50Ø]
Maryland. Constitutional Convention, 1967-1968.
   Proceedings of the Constitutional Convention of the
State, January 5-6, 1968.
   404 p.

[Md 50p]
Maryland. Constitutional Convention, 1967-1968.
   Proceedings of the Constitutional Convention of the
State, January 8, 10, 1968.
   223 p.

[Md 51]
Maryland. Constitutional Convention, 1967-1968.
   Journal of the Constitutional Convention of Maryland,
1967-1968. [Annapolis, 1968].
   xxii, 605 p.   illus.

[Md 52]
Maryland. Constitutional Convention, 1967-1968.
   Rules of the Constitutional Convention of Maryland, 1967.
Annapolis, State House, 1967.
   (2), 68 p.

[Md 53]
Maryland. Constitutional Convention Commission.
   Constitutional Revision Study Documents of the Constitu-
tional Convention Commission of Maryland, June 15, 1968.
[Annapolis] 1968.
   xxii, 1,188 pp   illus.

[Md 54]
Maryland. Constitutional Convention, 1967-1968.
   Comparison of the Present Constitution and the Constitution Proposed by the Convention, November 1, 1968. [Anna-
polis, 1968
   xxix, 252 p.

[Md 55]
Maryland.   Constitution.
     Constitution of Maryland with Amendments to January 1,
1973, and Constitution of the United States of America.
Edited by Department of Legislative Reference.   Secretary of
State of Maryland.   [Baltimore, 1973.]
     148 p.

Michigan

[Mi 21]
Citizen's Research Council of Michigan.
    Michigan's Constitutional Issues. Lansing, 1960.
    v.p.

[Mi 22A-S]
Michigan. Constitutional Convention, 1961-1962. Preparatory
    Committee.
    Michigan Constitutional Convention Studies. [Lansing]
1961.
    19 v.

[Mi 22A]
Michigan. Constitutional Convention, 1961-1962. Preparatory
    Committee.
    Constitutional Convention Study--The Meaning of American
Constitutional Government, by Alfred H. Kelly.

[Mi 22B]
Michigan. Constitutional Convention, 1961-1962. Preparatory
    Committee.
    Constitutional Convention Study--Constitutional Conven-
tion Powers, by William J. Pierce
    v, 27 p.

[Mi 22C]
Michigan. Constitutional Convention, 1961-1962. Preparatory
    Committee.
    Constitutional Convention Study--A Prepared Manual Of
Organization and Prodedure for A State Constitutional Conven-
tion, by William J. Pierce.
    v, 119 p.

[Mi 22D]
Michigan. Constitutional Convention, 1961-1962. Preparatory
    Committee.
    Constitutional Convention Study--Rejected Amendments to
the Michigan Constitution, 1910-1961, by Sidney Glazer.
    vi, 27 p.

[Mi 22E]
Michigan. Constitutional Convention, 1961-1962. Preparatory
    Committee.
    Constitutional Convention Study--The Declaration of Rights
in the Michigan Constitution, by Charles Shull.
    v, 12 p.

24

[Mi 22F]
Michigan. Constitutional Convention, 1961-1962. Preparatory
   Committee.
      Constitutional Convention Study--Elective Franchise and
the Michigan Constitution by, John P. White.
      v, 29 p.

[Mi 22G]
Michigan. Constitutional Convention, 1961-1962. Preparatory
   Committee.
      Constitutional Convention Study--The Constitution and the
Legislature, by Herbert Garfinkel.

[Mi 22H]
Michigan. Constitutional Convention, 1961-1962. Preparatory
   Committee.
      Constitutional Convention Study--The Executive and Civil
Service in the Michigan Constitution, by Albert L. Sturm and
Fred S. Steingold.
      vi, 38 p.

[Mi 22I]
Michigan. Constitutional Convention, 1961-1962. Preparatory
   Committee.
      Constitutional Convention Study--The Michigan Constitu-
tion and the Judiciary, by Charles W. Joiner.
      vi, 30 p.

[Mi 22J]
Michigan. Constitutional Convention, 1961-1962. Preparatory
   Committee.
      Constitutional Convention Study--Local Government and the
Michigan Constitution, by Louis L. Friedland.
      v, 52 p.

[Mi 22K]
Michigan. Constitutional Convention, 1961-1962. Preparatory
   Committee.
      Constitutional Convention Study--Elementary Education and
Secondary Education and The Michigan Constitution, by Donald
J. Leu.
      vi, 33 p.

[Mi 22L]
Michigan. Constitutional Convention, 1961-1962. Preparatory
   Committee.
      Constitutional Convention Study--Higher Education in
Michigan's Constitution, by Willis F. Dunbar.
      vi, 24 p.

[Mi 22M]
Michigan. Constitutional Convention, 1961-1962. Preparatory
   Committee.
      Constitutional Convention Study--Taxation and Fiscal
Policy in the Michigan Constitution, by Raleigh Barlowe.
      v, 44 p.

[Mi 22N]
Michigan. Constitutional Convention, 1961-1962. Preparatory
  Committee.
    Constitutional Convention Study--The Michigan Constitution
and Eminent Domain, by Solomon Bienenfeld.
    iv, 16 p.

[Mi 22Ø]
Michigan. Constitutional Convention, 1961-1962. Preparatory
  Committee.
    Constitutional Convention Study--State Constitutional
Provisions on Exemptions, by Robert E. Childs.
    v, 25 p.

[Mi 22P]
Michigan. Constitutional Convention, 1961-1962. Preparatory
  Committee.
    Constitutional Convention Study--Corporations and the
Michigan Constitution, by Alfred F. Conrad, Richard W. Ogders,
and Timothy F. Scanlon.
    v.p.

[Mi 22Q]
Michigan. Constitutional Convention, 1961-1962. Preparatory
  Committee.
    Constitutional Convention Study--Direct Government in
Michigan: Initiative, Referendum, Recall and Revision in the
Michigan Constitution, by Daniel S. McHargue.
    vi, 116 p.

[Mi 22R]
Michigan. Constitutional Convention, 1961-1962. Preparatory
  Committee.
    Constitutional Convention Study--Miscellaneous Problems:
Boundaries, by George S. May; Impeachment and Removal in
Michigan, by Charles W. Joiner and Jon F. DeWitt; Memorandum
Concerning Article XVI of the Michigan Constitution, by
Charles W. Joiner and Jon F. DeWitt.
    v, 30 p.

[Mi 22S]
Michigan. Constitutional Convention, 1961-1962. Preparatory
  Committee.
    Constitutional Convention Study--An Advance Directory of
Delegates for the Michigan Constitutional Convention Convened
October 3, 1961.
    iv, 14 p.

[Mi 23]
Michigan. Constitution.
    Constitution of the State of Michigan. Secretary of
State. Lansing, 1961.
    66 p.

[Mi 24]
Michigan. Constitutional Convention, 1961-1962.
    Handbook of the Michigan Constitutional Convention.
Lansing, 1962.
    68 p.

[Mi 25]
Michigan. Constitutional Convention, 1961-1962.
    Committee Proposals of the Constitutional Convention,
Numbers 1-129. Lansing, 1962.
    2 v.

[Mi 26]
Michigan. Constitutional Convention, 1961-1962.
    Delegate Proposals of the Constitutional Convention,
Numbers 1001-1830. Lansing, 1962.
    2 v.

[Mi 27]
Michigan. Constitutional Convention, 1961-1962.
    Exclusion Reports of the Constitutional Convention,
Numbers 2001-2046. Lansing, 1962.
    v.p.

[Mi 28A-N]
Michigan. Constitutional Convention, 1961-1962.
    Action Journal, Hearings and Calendars of the Constitu-
tional Convention. Lansing, 1962.
    14 v.

[Mi 28A]
Michigan. Constitutional Convention, 1961-1962.
    Action Journal, Hearings and Calendars--Volume 1, Admin-
istration.
    v.p.

[Mi 28B]
Michigan. Constitutional Convention, 1961-1962.
    Action Journal, Hearings and Calendars--Volume 2, Declar-
ation of Rights, Suffrage and Elections.
    v.p.

[Mi 28C]
Michigan. Constitutional Convention, 1961-1962.
    Action Journal, Hearings and Calendars--Volume 3, Educa-
tion.
    v.p.

[Mi 28D]
Michigan. Constitutional Convention, 1961-1962.
    Action Journal, Hearings and Calendars--Volume 4, Emerg-
ing Problems.
    v.p.

[Mi 28E]
Michigan. Constitutional Convention, 1961-1962.
    Action Journal, Hearings and Calendars--Volume 5, xecu-
tive Branch.
    v.p.

[Mi 28F]
Michigan. Constitutional Convention, 1961-1962.
    Action Journal, Hearings and Calendars--Volume 6, Finance
and Taxation.
    v.p.

[Mi 28G]
Michigan. Constitutional Convention, 1961-1962.
    Action Journal, Hearings and Calendars--Volume 7, Judi-
cial Branch.
    v.p.

[Mi 28H]
Michigan. Constitutional Convention, 1961-1962.
    Action Journal, Hearings and Calendars--Volume 8, Legis-
lative Organization.
    v.p.

[Mi 28I]
Michigan. Constitutional Convention, 1961-1962.
    Action Journal, Hearings and Calendars--Volume 9, Legis-
lative Powers.
    v.p.

[Mi 28J]
Michigan. Constitutional Convention, 1961-1962.
    Action Journal, Hearings and Calendars--Volume 10, Local
Government.
    v.p.

[Mi 28K]
Michigan. Constitutional Convention, 1961-1962.
    Action Journal, Hearings and Calendars--Volume 11, Mis-
cellaneous Provisions & Schedule.
    v.p.

[Mi 28L]
Michigan. Constitutional Convention, 1961-1962.
    Action Journal, Hearings and Calendars--Volume 12, Public
Information.
    v.p.

[Mi 28M]
Michigan. Constitutional Convention, 1961-1962.
    Action Journal, Hearings and Calendars--Volume 13, Rules
& Resolutions.
    v.p.

[Mi 28N]
Michigan. Constitutional Convention, 1961-1962.
    Action Journal, Hearings and Calendars--Volume 14, Style
and Drafting.
    v.p.

[Mi 29]
Michigan. Constitutional Convention, 1961-1962.
    Final Convention Calendar of the 1961-1962 Michigan Con-
stitutional Convention. Lansing, 1962.
    v.p.

[Mi 30]
Michigan. Constitutional Convention, 1961-1962.
    Status of Proposals of the Constitutional Convention.
Lansing, 1962.
    v.p.

[Mi 31]
Michigan. Constitutional Convention, 1961-1962.
    Offic al Record of the Constitutional Convention of the
State of Michigan. Lansing, 1962.
    2 v.

[Mi 32]
Michigan. Constitutional Convention, 1961-1962.
    Journal of the Constitutional Convention of the State of
Michigan. Lansing, 1962.
    2 v.

[Mi 33]
Citizen's Research Council of Michigan.
    Report No. 212: The Proposed Constitution: A Comparison
with the Present Constitution. Detroit, 1962.
    v.p.

[Mi 34]
Michigan. Constitution.
    The Constitution of the State of Michigan. [Secretary
of State. Lansing, 1963.]
    64 p.

Montana

[Mon 7]
Montana. Constitutional Convention Commission.
    Montana Constitutional Convention Studies, #3, The Constitution of Montana and the Constitution of the United States with indexes. [Helena] n.d.
    vi, 150 p.
    At head of title: Montana Constitutional Convention, 1971-1972.

[Mon 8]
Montana. Constitution.
    The Montana Constitution, a Report to the Forty-First Legislative Assembly by the Montana Legislative Council, October, 1968. [Helena, 1968]
    ix, 95 p.

[Mon 9-18]
Montana. Constitutional Convention Commission.
    Montana Constitutional Convention Studies [Helena] n.d.
    10 volumes
    At head of title: Montana Constitutional Convention, 1971-1972.

[Mon 9]
Montana. Constitutional Convention Commission.
    Convention Study #7, Constitutional Provisions Proposed by the Constitution Revision Commission Subcommittees.
    iv, 188 p.

[Mon 10]
Montana. Constitutional Convention Commission.
    Convention Study #10, The Bill of Rights by Rick Applegate.
    x, 425 p.

[Mon 11]
Montana. Constitutional Convention Commission.
    Convention Study #11, Suffrage and Election by James Grady.
    vi, 133 p.

[Mon 12]
Montana. Constitutional Convention Commission.
    Convention Study #12, The Legislature by Richard F. Bechtel.
    vi, 174p.

[Mon 13]
Montana. Constitutional Convention Commission.
    Convention Study #13, The Executive by Karen Beck.
    viii, 232 p.

[Mon 14]
Montana. Constitutional Convention Commission.
    Convention Study #14, The Judiciary by Sandra R. Muck-
leston.
    viii, 349 p.   illus.

[Mon 15]
Montana. Constitutional Convention Commission.
    Convention Study #15, Taxation and Finance by Roger A.
Barber.
    xii, 410 p.   illus.

[Mon 16]
Montana. Constitutional Convention Commission.
    Convention Study #16, Local Government by Jerry R.
Holloron.
    viii, 328 p.

[Mon 17]
Montana. Constitutional Convention Commission.
    Convention Study #17, Education by Bruce Sievers.
    vi, 254 p.

[Mon 18]
Montana. Constitutional Convention Commission.
    Convention Study #1, Constitutional Convention Enabling
Act.
    vi, 75 p.   illus.

[Mon 19A-
Montana. Constitutional Convention, 1971-1972.
    Transcript of Proceedings of the Montana Constitutional
Convention, 1971-1972 [held] November 29, 1971 [- March 24,
1972, at] Convention Hall, State Capitol. Helena [1972].
    12 v
-- ---Index to the Proceedings. Helena [1972]. 34 l.

[Mon 19A]
Montana. Constitutional Convention, 1971-1972.
    Proceedings of the Constitutional Convention of the
State, November 29 to December 1, 1971.
    368 p.

[Mon 19B]
Montana. Constitutional Convention, 1971-1972.
    Proceedings of the Constitutional Convention of the
State, January 17 to February 4, 1972.
    663 p.

[Mon 19C]
Montana. Constitutional Convention, 1971-1972.
   Proceedings of the Constitutional Convention of the
State, February 5 to February 18, 1972.
   626 p.

[Mon 19D]
Montana. Constitutional Convention, 1971-1972.
   Proceedings of the Constitutional Convention of the
State, February 19 to February 23, 1972.
   837 p.

[Mon 19E]
Montana. Constitutional Convention, 1971-1972.
   Proceedings of the Constitutional Convention of the
State, February 24 to February 25, 1972.
   553 p.

[Mon 19F]
Montana. Constitutional Convention, 1971-1972.
   Proceedings of the Constitutional Convention of the
State, February 26 to March 1, 1972.
   871 p.

[Mon 19G]
Montana. Constitutional Convention, 1971-1972.
   Proceedings of the Constitutional Convention of the
State, March 2 to March 5, 1972.
   900 p.

[Mon 19H]
Montana. Constitutional Convention, 1971-1972.
   Proceedings of the Constitutional Convention of the
State, March 7 to March 9, 1972.
   900 p.

[Mon 19I]
Montana. Constitutional Convention, 1971-1972.
   Proceedings of the Constitutional Convention of the
State, March 10 to March 11, 1972.
   688 p.

[Mon 19J]
Montana. Constitutional Convention, 1971-1972.
   Proceedings of the Constitutional Convention of the
State, March 13 to March 14, 1972.
   637 p.

[Mon 19K]
Montana. Constitutional Convention, 1971-1972.
   Proceedings of the Constitutional Convention of the
State, March 15 to March 16, 1972.
   722 p.

[Mon 19L]
Montana. Constitutional Convention, 1971-1972.
    Proceedings of the Constitutional Convention of the
State, March 17 to March 18, 1972.
    661 p.

[Mon 19M]
Montana. Constitutional Convention, 1971-1972.
    Proceedings of the Constitutional Convention of the
State, March 20 to March 24, 1974.
    861 p.

[Mon 19N]
Montana. Constitutional Convention, 1971-1972.
    Index to the Proceedings to the Constitutional Convention
of the State, November 29, 1971 to March 24, 1972.
    39 l.

[Mon 20]
Montana. Constitution.
    Constitution of the State of Montana, as Adopted by the
Constitutional Convention, March 22, 1972 and as Ratified by
the People June 6, 1972. Frank Murray, Secretary of State,
Helena, 1972.
    iv, 66 p.

New Hampshire

[NH 35]
New Hampshire. Commission to Study the State Constitution.
    Report to the Fifteenth Constitutional Convention by the
Commission to Study the State Constitution. Joseph A. Milli-
met, Chariman. [Concord, 1963 or 4
    30 p.

[NH 36]
New Hampshire. Constitutional Convention, 1964.
    Convention to Revise the Constitution. [Concord] 1964.
    414 p.

[NH 37]
New Hampshire. Constitution.
    The Constitution of New Hampshire. [Concord, Office of
the Secretary of State, 1973?].
    [52] p.

New Jersey

[NJ 21]
New Jersey. Constitutional Convention, 1966.
[Background Papers of the 1966 Constitutional Convention
of the State of New Jersey. Trenton, 1966.]
v.p.

CONTENTS: Background of the Constitutional Convention,
by A. B. Handler. Single-member v. Multi-member Districts,
by E. M. Matthews. Present Legislative Organization, Des-
cription and Prepresentation Analysis, by S. A. Alito. The
Prevention of Gerrymandering, by E. C. Roeck, Jr. Retaining
Counties as Legislative Districts, by C. S. Cummis. Size of
the Legislature, by R. G. Smith. Non-population Factors in
Legislative Districting, by R. A. Hogarty. Allowable and De-
sirable Population Deviations, by E. C. Roeck, Jr. Methods
for Future Apportionment or Redistricting, by V. P. Biunno.
Unicameralism v. Bicameralism, by N. A. McDonald. The Use
of Congressional Districts as Legislative Districts, by R. J.
Connors.

[NJ 22]
New Jersey. Constitution.
Constitution of the State of New Jersey, as Amended to
January 1, 1974. Trenton, 1974.
48 p.

"Published under the authority of the Department of
State."

New Mexico

[NM 13]
New Mexico. Constitutional Revision Commission.
    Report of the Constitutional Revision Commission, State
of New Mexico to [the] Honorable David F. Cargo, Governor of
New Mexico and to Members of the Twenty-Eighth Legislature of
the State of New Mexico. [Santa Fe, 1967].
    v, 261 p.

[NM 14]
New Mexico. Constitutional Convention, 1969.
    New Mexico Constitutional Convention, August 5, 1969.
[Santa Fe] Ernestine D. Evans, Secretary of State [1969].
    85 p.

    CONTENTS: Enabling Act of the 1969 Constitutional Con-
vention; Election Results from the State Election Districts;
Short Biographies of the 70 Constitutional Convention Delegates.

[NM 15]
New Mexico. Constitution.
    The Constitution of the State of New Mexico; as adopted
January 21, 1911, and as subsequently amended by the People
in General and Special Elections 1912 through 1974. [Santa
Fe] Ernestine D. Evans, Secretary of State, January 1975.
    96 p.

New York

[NY 56-71]
New York (State). Temporary State Commission on the Constitutional Convention.
   Reports. New York City, 1967.
   16 volumes

[NY 56]
New York (State). Temporary State Commission on the Constitutional Convention.
   Report #1--1967 Convention Issues: Introductory Report.
   78 p.

[NY 57]
New York (State). Temporary State Commission on the Constitutional Convention.
   Report #2--Toward an Effective Convention: Legislature and Other Recommendations.
   72 p.

[NY 58]
New York (State). Temporary State Commission on the Constitutional Convention.
   Report #3--Local Finance.
   178 p.

[NY 59]
New York (State). Temporary State Commission on the Constitutional Convention.
   Report #4--The Right to Vote.
   83 p.

[NY 60]
New York (State). Temporary State Commission on the Constitutional Convention.
   Report #5--For Effective Constitutional Review: Convention Organization and Rules.
   48 p.

[NY 61]
New York (State). Temporary State Commission on the Constitutional Convention.
   Report #6--Education.
   90 p.

[NY 62]
New York (State). Temporary State Commission on the Constitutional Convention.
   Report #7--Individual Liberties.
   211 p.

[NY 63]
New York (State). Temporary State Commission on the Constitutional Convention.
   Report #8--State Finance.
   186 p.

[NY 64]
New York (State). Temporary State Commission on the Constitutional Convention.
   Report #9--Housing, Labor and Natural Resources.
   119 p.

[NY 65]
New York (State). Temporary State Commission on the Constitutional Convention.
   Report #10--Individual Freedoms.
   67 p.

[NY 66]
New York (State). Temporary State Commission on the Consti-
tutional Convention.
   Report #11--Social Services: Welfare, Health and Mental
Health.
   103 p.

[NY 67]
New York (State). Temporary State Commission on the Constitutional Convention.
   Report #12--Judiciary.
   292 p.

[NY 68]
New York (State). Temporary State Commission on the Constitutional Convention.
   Report #13--Local Government.
   150 p.

[NY 69]
New York (State). Temporary State Commission on the Constitutional Convention.
   Report #14--State Government.
   227 p.

[NY 70]
New York (State). Temporary State Commission on the Consti-
tutional Convention.
   Report #15--Final Report: Constitutional Revision and
Simplification.
   35 p.

[NY 71]
New York (State). Temporary State Commission on the Constitutional Convention.
   Report #16--Index.
   18 p.

[NY 72A-E]
New York (State). Department of Audit and Control.
   Comptroller's Studies for the 1967 Constitutional Convention. [Albany], 1967.
   5 volumes

[NY 72A]
New York (State). Department of Audit and Control.
   Comptroller's Study--Tax Limits of Counties, Cities and Villages, 1963-1967.
   44 p.

[NY 72B]
New York (State). Department of Audit and Control.
   Comptroller's Study--New York State Fiscal Affairs and Debt Structure.
   v.p.

[NY 72C]
New York (State). Department of Audit and Control.
   Comptroller's Study--Tax Limits of School Districts in Cities, 1952-1967.
   v.p.

[NY 72D]
New York (State). Department of Audit and Control.
   Comptroller's Study--Public Authorities in New York State: A Financial Study.
   66 p.

[NY 72E]
New York (State). Department of Audit and Control.
   Comptroller's Study--Constitutional Limitations on Municipal Debt.
   105 p.

[NY 73]
New York (State). Constitution.
   The Constitution of the State of New York, as revised, with amendments adopted by the Constitutional Convention of 1938 and approved by vote of the people on November 8, 1938, as amended and in force January 1, 1967.
   267 p.

[NY 74]
New York (State). Constitutional Convention, 1967.
   Rules of the 1967 New York State Constitutional Convention and Pertinent Resolutions and Statutes. [Albany, 1967].
   55 p.

[NY 75A-F]
New York (State). Constitutional Convention, 1967.
　　Proceedings of the Constitutional Convention of the
State of New York, April 14-September 26, 1967. [Albany],
1967.
　　12 volumes

[NY 75A]
New York (State). Constitutional Convention, 1967.
　　Proceedings of the Constitutional Convention--Directory
of Delegates.
　　168 p.

[NY 75B]
New York (State). Constitutional Convention, 1967.
　　Proceedings of the Constitutional Convention--Record of
Proceedings.
　　3 volumes

[NY 75C]
New York (State). Constitutional Convention, 1967.
　　Proceedings of the Constitutional Convention--Journal,
Calendars and Resolutions.
　　v.p.

[NY 75]
New York (State). Constitutional Convention, 1967.
　　Proceedings of the Constitutional Convention--Proposi-
tions.
　　5 volumes

[NY 75E]
New York (State). Constitutional Convention, 1967.
　　Proceedings of the Constitutional Convention--Documents.
　　v.p.

[NY 75F]
New York (State). Constitutional Convention, 1967.
　　Proceedings of the Constitutional Convention--Index.
　　vii, 330 p.

[NY 76]
New York (State). Constitutional Convention, 1967.
　　Text, Abstract and Highlights of Proposed Constitution
of the State of New York to be Submitted to the Electors of
the State, November 7, 1967. [Albany], 1967.
　　xv, 73 p.

[NY 77]
New York (State). Constitution.
    The Constitution of the State of New York, as revised,
with Amendments Adopted by the Constitutional Convention of
1938 and Approved by the Vote of the People on November 8,
1938 and Amendments Subsequently Adopted by the Legislature
and Approved by Vote of the People During the Years 1939-
1969, Inclusive. [As Amended and in Force, January 1, 1970.
Albany]. John P. Lomenzo, Secretary of State. [1970?]
    7, 349 p.

North Dakota

[ND 8]
North Dakota. Constitutional Convention, 1971-1972.
    Constitution of the State of North Dakota with all Amend-
ments Adopted to and Including January 1, 1971. Bismark,
Department of Public Instruction [1971].
    v.p.

[ND 9]
North Dakota. Constitutional Convention Delegates.
    Resource Publication C: Convention Profile and Indivi-
dual Biographies by Boyd L. Wright and Lloyd A. Bakken.
Grand Forks: University of North Dakota, Bureau of Governmental Affairs, 1971.
    102 p.

[ND 10]
North Dakota. Constitutional Convention, 1971-1972.
    Interim Report [of the] North Dakota Constitutional Con-
vention. [Bismark, 1971].
    vii, 112 p.

[ND 11]
North Dakota. Constitutional Convention, 1971-1972.
    Debates of the North Dakota Constitutional Convention of
1972. Published by authority of the North Dakota Constitutional Convention of 1972. [Bismark, 1972].
    2 volumes

[ND 12]
North Dakota. Constitutional Convention, 1971-1972.
    Journal: North Dakota Constitutional Convention, 1971-
1972. Frank A. Wenstrom, President; Roy Gilbreath, Chief
Clerk. Bismark, 1972.
    xv, 679 p.

[ND 13]
North Dakota. Constitution.
    The Constitution of the State of North Dakota, as amended
to July 1, 1973 [including 1975 supplement]. [Bismark] Secretary of State, 1975.
    n.p.

Pennsylvania

[Pa 25]
Pennsylvania Bar Association. Committee on Constitutional
  Revision.
    Report: Project Constitution, March 9, 1959. [Harris-
burg, 1959].
    226 p.

[Pa 26]
Pennsylvania Bar Association.
    "Project Constitution Sub-Committee Reports." Pennsyl-
vania Bar Association Quarterly 33 (June 1962): 378-498.

[Pa 27]
Pennsylvania Bar Association.
    "A Revised Constitution for Pennsylvania: Project Con-
stitution." Pennsylvania Bar Association Quarterly 34
(January 1963, no. 2A).
    iv, 147-325 p.

[Pa 28]
Pennsylvania Bar Association.
    Highlights of the Twelve Resolutions Presented to the
1963 Pennsylvania Legislature by the Pennsylvania Bar Association Which Would Constitute a Revised State Constitution.
    35 p.

[Pa 29]
Pennsylvania Bar Association. Special Committee on Project
  Constitution.
    Report, December 1964. Harrisburg, 1964.
    xii, 74 p.

    Reports of the committees and sub-committees of the
Special Committee on Project Constitution of the Pennsylvania
Bar Association.

[Pa 30]
Pennsylvania Bar Association.
    A Revised Constitution for Pennsylvania: Project Con-
stitution, December 17, 1963. [Harrisburg] 1963.
    xi, 89 p.

    "Twelve resolutions submitted to the Governor's Commis-
sion on Constitutional Revision by the Pennsylvania Bar
Association."

[Pa 31]
Pennsylvania. Governor's Commission on Constitutional
   Revision.
   Report with Recommendations of Resolutions to be Intro-
duced Into the General Assembly. [Harrisburg] 1964.
   99 p.

[Pa 32]
Pennsylvania Economy League, Inc.
   Comparison of Proposed New Constitutional Provisions with
Pennsylvania's Present Constitution [revised edition, July
1965]. Harrisburg [1965].
   110 p.

   "The first edition was published in April 1965. The
Senate having approved the proposed amendments, with some
modification, this edition contains the proposals as adopted
by the Senate."

[Pa 33]
Pennsylvania Bar Association. Special Committee on Project
   Constitution.
   Report to the Annual Meeting, January 1966. Pittsburgh,
1966.
   iii, 45 p.

[Pa 34]
Pennsylvania Bar Association.
   Proposals to the Preparatory Committee and the Constitutional Convention. Harrisburg, 1967.
   vi, 78 p.

   "Authorized by the voters of Pennsylvania under Act No.
2 of the 1967 Session of the Legislature with introductory
note, comments on the several proposals and statement regard-
ing the proposed Judiciary article."

[Pa 35]
Pennsylvania Bar Association.
   Pennsylvania Constitutional Revision: 1966 Handbook.
Harrisburg, 1966.
   101 p.

[Pa 36]
Pennsylvania. Constitution.
   Constitution of the Commonwealth of Pennsylvania, as
amended by Majority Vote of the Electors in 1965, 1966,
1967. [Harrisburg, 1967].
   42 l.

[Pa 37]
Pennsylvania. Constitutional Convention, 1967-1968. Preparatory Committee.
   Testimony at Public Hearings and Other Statements. [Har-
risburg, 1967].
   v.p.

[Pa 38-46]
Pennsylvania. Constitutional Convention, 1967-1968. Pre-
    paratory Committee.
    Reference Manual. [Harrisburg, 1967].
    9 volumes

[Pa 38]
Pennsylvania. Constitutional Convention, 1967-1968. Pre-
    paratory Committee.
    Reference Manual #1 -- The Convention.
    81 p.

[Pa 39]
Pennsylvania. Constitutional Convention, 1967-1968. Pre-
    paratory Committee.
    Reference Manual #2 -- Constitution of Pennsylvania
and [the] Constitution of the United States.
    388 p.

[Pa 40]
Pennsylvania. Constitutional Convention, 1967-1968. Pre-
    paratory Committee.
    Reference Manual #3 -- A History of Pennsylvania Consti-
tutions.
    38 p.

[Pa 41]
Pennsylvania. Constitutional Convention, 1967-1968. Pre-
    paratory Committee.
    Reference Manual #4 -- Local Government.
    288 p.

[Pa 42]
Pennsylvania. Constitutional Convention, 1967-1968. Pre-
    paratory Committee.
    Reference Manual #5 -- The Judiciary.
    435 p.

[Pa 43]
Pennsylvania. Constitutional Convention, 1967-1968. Pre-
    paratory Committee.
    Reference Manual #6 -- Legislative Apportionment.
    108 p.

[Pa 44]
Pennsylvania. Constitutional Convention, 1967-1968. Pre-
    paratory Committee.
    Reference Manual #7 -- Taxation and State Finance.
    76 p.

[Pa 45]
Pennsylvania. Constitutional Convention, 1967-1968. Pre-
    paratory Committee.
    Reference Manual #8 -- Bibliography by Florence C.
Steigerwalt.
    28 p.

[Pa 46]
Pennsylvania. Constitutional Convention, 1967-1968. Preparatory Committee.
    Reference Manual #9 -- Index.
    84 p.

[Pa 47]
Pennsylvania. Constitutional Convention, 1967-1968.
    Debates of the Pennsylvania Constitutional Convention
of 1967-1968. Harrisburg, 1969.
    2 volumes.

[Pa 48]
Pennsylvania. Constitutional Convention, 1967-1968.
    Delegate Proposals, Numbers 1000 to 1209. [Harrisburg,
1968].
    v.p.

[Pa 49]
Pennsylvania. Constitution.
    Constitution of the Commonwealth of Pennsylvania, 1972.
General Assembly, Commonwealth of Pennsylvania [Harrisburg]
1972.
    66 p.

Rhode Island

[RI 26]
Rhode Island. Special Commission To Make a Comprehensive
   Examination of the Constitution of the State.
   Report of the Commission on Revision of the Rhode
Island Constitution, submitted to the Governor and General
Assembly, September 1962 [Providence?, 1962].
   139 p.

[RI 27]
Rhode Island. Constitution.
   Constitution and Charter: State of Rhode Island and
Providence Plantations. [Providence]. Prepared and
distributed by August P. LaFrance, Secretary of State
[196-].
   76 p.

[RI 28]
Rhode Island. Constitutional Convention, 1964-1969.
   Report of the Proceedings of the Convention, December
8, 1964 to February 17, 1969. Dennis J. Roberts, Chairman.
[Providence, 1969].
   3 volumes

[RI 29]
Rhode Island. Constitutional Convention, 1973.
   The Proceedings of the Rhode Island Constitutional
Convention of 1973. [Compiled and edited by Patrick T.
Conley. Providence, 1973].
   159 p.

[RI 30]
Rhode Island. Constitution.
   Constitution and Charter, State of Rhode Island and
Providence Plantations. Prepared and distributed by
Robert F. Burnes, Secretary of State, 1975.
   81 p.

Tennessee

[Tn 14]
Tennessee. Legislature.
 Public Acts at Extraordinary Session, 1962. Chapter 2.
 6 p. (enabling legislation).

[Tn 15]
Tennessee. Legislative Council Committee.
 Information Concerning Tennessee's Limited Constitutional
Convention to Convene July 26, 1965. State Capitol, Nashville. Prepared for members of the General Assembly and
others. [Nashville, 1965].
 8 leaves

[Tn 16]
Tennessee. Constitutional Convention, 1965.
 Journal and Debates of the Limited Constitutional Con-
vention of the State of Tennessee, July 26-December 10, 1965.
[Nashville, 1966].
 v.p.

[Tn 17]
Tennessee. Legislature.
 Acts of 1968. Chapter 421.
 10 p.

[Tn 18]
Tennessee. Constitutional Convention, 1971.
 Journal and Debates of the Limited Constitutional Convention of the State of Tennessee, August 2-September 15,
1971. [Nashville, 1974].
 v.p.

[Tn 19]
Prescott, Frank William.
 Journal and Proceedings, Constitutional Convention,
State of Tennessee, 1971--Errata. [Chattanooga, 1974].
 11 p.

[Tn 20]
Tennessee. Constitution.
 "Constitution of the State of Tennessee, as amended."
Tennessee Blue Book, 1973-1974; Rita A. Whitfield, editor.
Issued by the Office of the Secretary of State. Nashville,
1973.
 369-390 p.

Texas

[Tx 27]
Texas. Constitutional Revision Commission.
    Report and Recommended Revised Constitution to the Members of the 61<u>st</u> Legislature. Austin, 1968.
    xv, 224 leaves

[Tx 28]
Texas. Joint Con titutional Convention Planning Commission.
    Proposed Rules of Procedure: 1974 Texas Constitutional Convention. Austin, 1971.
    [3], 72 p.

[Tx 29]
Bebout, John E.
    The Texas Constitution: Problems and Prospects for Revision. Papers prepared for the Texas Urban Development Commission by John E. Bebout and Janice C. May. Arlington [Institute of Urban Studies, University of Texas at Arlington] 1971.
    v, 98 p.

    "The Problems of the Texas Constitution" by John E. Bebout and "Constitutional Revision in Texas" by Janice C. May.

[Tx 30]
Texas. Constitution.
    Constitution of the State of Texas (adopted February 15, 1876). Austin, Texas Advisory Commission on Intergovernmental Relations, [1972].
    v, 160 p.

    A reconstruction of the Constitution of Texas including all amendments since 1876..."most accurate rendition of the Constitution available."

[Tx 31]
Braden, George D.
    Citizen's Guide to the Texas Constitution. [Austin] Texas Advisory Commission on Intergovernmental Relations, [1972].
    viii, 95 p.

[Tx 32]
Texas. Advisory Commission on Intergovernmental Relations.
     The Texas Constitutional Revision Commission of 1973:
a Report and Proposal of the Commission. Austin, 1972.
     v, 38 p.

[Tx 33]
Texas. Constitutional Revision Commission.
     A New Constitution for Texas. Prepared by the Commission
Austin, 1973.
     vii, 51 p.

[Tx 34]
Texas. Constitutional Revision Commission.
     A New Constitution for Texas: Text, Explanation and
Commentary. Prepared by the Commission. Austin, 1973.
     vii, 226 p.

[Tx 35]
Texas. Constitutional Revision Commission.
     A New Constitution for Texas: Separate Statements of
Commission Members. Austin, 1973.
     vii, 48 p.

[Tx 36]
Texas. Advisory Commission on Intergovernmental Relations.
     The Texas Constitution: A Reorganization and Simplifi-
cation Without Substantive Change. Austin, 1973.
     v.p.

[Tx 37]
Texas. Joint Constitutional Convention Planning Commission.
     Staff Reports: 1974 Texas Constitutional Convention.
Austin, 1974.
     iii, 52 p.

[Tx 38]
Texas. Joint Constitutional Convention Planning Commission.
     Final Report to the Delegates: 1974 Constitutional Con-
vention. Austin, 1974.
     xix, 53 p.

[Tx 39]
Texas. Constitutional Revision Commission.
     The Texas Constitution: An Annotated and Comparative
Analysis, preliminary edition. Austin, 1974.
     3 volumes

[Tx 40]
Texas. Constitutional Revision Commission.
     Resolution for Submission of the Proposals of the Con-
vention to the Qualified Electors of the State, number 32.
As reported by the Committee on Submission and Transition.
Austin, 1974.